ROAD TRIPS

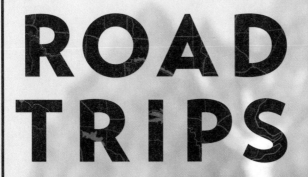

ROAD TRIPS

A GUIDE TO TRAVEL, ADVENTURE, AND CHOOSING YOUR OWN PATH

Jen CK Jacobs

ROOST BOOKS | BOULDER | 2018

ROOST BOOKS

An imprint of Shambhala Publications, Inc.
4720 Walnut Street
Boulder, Colorado 80301
roostbooks.com

Text and photos © 2018 by Jen CK Jacobs
Photos on pages 45 and 47 © 2018
by Lisa Congdon
Photos on page vi (background),
48 © 2018 by Ann-Kathrin Koch
Photos on page 33, 53
© 2018 by Heidi Swanson

9 8 7 6 5 4 3 2 1
First Edition
Printed in the United States of America

♾ This edition is printed on acid-free paper
that meets the American National Stan-
dards Institute Z39.48 Standard.

♻ Shambhala Publications makes every
effort to print on recycled paper. For more information please visit www.shambhala.com.

Distributed in the United States by
Penguin Random House LLC and in Canada
by Random House of Canada Ltd

Designed by Daniel Urban-Brown

LIBRARY OF CONGRESS CATALOGING-IN-PUBLICATION DATA

Names: Jacobs, Jen CK, author.
Title: Road trips: a guide to travel,
adventure, and choosing your own path
/ Jen CK Jacobs.
Description: First edition.
| Boulder, Colorado: Roost Books, 2018.
Identifiers: LCCN 2017009888 | ISBN
9781611802030 (pbk.: alk. paper)
Subjects: LCSH: Automobile travel. |
Jacobs, Jen CK—Travel.
Classification: LCC GV1021 .J32 2018 |
DDC 796.7—dc23
LC record available at https://lccn.loc.
gov/2017009888

CONTENTS

RAGO
Inn

B

SFO ~]

LEFT SF
AS IT SHO
ABOUT T
AND PRETTI
LOVE THIS
WITH JETBU
LISTENING
AT CLOUD
THEN AN

Pari

DG |

TO T
T S
ASTA
COU
ORANGE
FLEE
S

INTRODUCTION:
WHY WE ROAD TRIP

MOST OF US CAN identify at least one book that changed our lives. If you're an avid reader, chances are high that more than one novel forever altered your way of seeing the world around you. For me, there were three such books. The first was Marion Zimmer Bradley's *The Mists of Avalon*—a sweeping saga of the Arthurian legend from the perspective of the most powerful women of the time. Not only did the novel spark a fire for the love of old-world magic and the country of England, but it was my initial encounter with truly formidable female protagonists. I felt empowered as a young woman for the first time in my life. The second book was *Skinny Legs and All* by Tom Robbins, an almost-fairy tale of love and philosophy in which a can of beans, a conch shell, and a spoon play vital roles. His words coaxed me to see the world as an evolving being, full of its own energy and angst. Robbins ripped off the proverbial Band-Aid of my myopic youth and demanded that I look at those around me with a deeper understanding and greater empathy.

But it was Jack Kerouac's *On the Road* that influenced my life path the most. Kerouac's straight-as-an-arrow prose stabbed my heart and made me realize the possibilities of what travel can do to our souls, how it alters us, how it forces us to evolve and often face truths once outside our comfort zones. I wrote out quotes from his book in my journals, taped them to my wall, and scribbled them on my arm. Kerouac spoke to the woman I was aching to become: independent, critical of the ideals and philosophies that funneled us into prescribed designs of adulthood, and, most inspiring, a traveler. I channeled his haunting energy as I hitched a U-Haul to the back of my Jeep in 1995 and drove from the cornfields of Nebraska, up and over the blanketed Rocky Mountains, and down into the dusty desert before reaching the golden shores of Southern California. I was twenty years old and had taken numerous drives across the United States in both directions with my parents before that trip. But this was different. This was my *On the Road*.

My taste for that type of travel never really died. Throughout my life I have continued to choose travel by car over air. As my children were born, that still seemed to me a more obvious choice. Friends could not believe that I would put my three girls in the back seat of my truck and drive halfway across the country—and actually enjoy it. But you miss everything—all of the real stuff—when 40,000 feet above ground. The rolling fields that still echo of battle cries; the ghosts of our forebearers haunting historic landmarks; the brick streets and soda fountain soul of Main Street, USA; the way the Rocky Mountains rise from the Great Plains as if waking an ancient beast from a long slumber; the diversity of people, architecture, and food. All of these experiences can be found behind the wheel. There is an old adage that travel changes you. In what way? Well, in absolutely every

way. Our lives should not be made up of what we physically accumulate, but by our shared experiences. Giving ourselves and our children the opportunity to see life outside of the proverbial bubble is not only transformative as a person and a parent, but it teaches us that the world is a big, beautiful, multifaceted evolving entity—one we will care about deeply if given the opportunity to explore her depths.

Additionally, there is something all at once nostalgic about taking road trips. Whether your first was fighting with your sibling in the backseat while you crossed state lines to your grandparents' house or a getaway with your significant other or best friend—it's likely a memory you'll never forget. This book celebrates those memories and encourages you to create new ones with your family or friends, and even on your own. The book you are now holding in your hands is meant to serve as a tome of inspiration, but I've included some practical pointers for your next trip as well. Part 1 gives you an overview of the road basics—a crash course of sorts in preparing your car, luggage, and route to ensure a safe and organized trip. Part 2 covers the importance of recording your travels—whether in a journal or with a camera—shares thoughts about chronicling in a new way, and provides ideas for writing prompts. Part 3 is the heart of the book. Reading as if pages from my own journals, I share some of my recent travels with you. I spent a week in February alone in the desert, crossing from the blinding lights of Los Angeles into the stark beauty of Joshua Tree; my best friend and I drove the coast of Ireland during a particularly glittering June; and I piled all those aforementioned babies into my truck and explored the wilds of Wyoming and Montana on an epic all-American road trip. I share with you photographs, thoughts, and recipes inspired by dishes discovered along the way. You'll also find a story about a recent day trip with tips and inspiration to simply get out of the house for the day—you don't have to map a course across state lines to experience the thrill of escapism. Part 4 is about bringing the road home with you—how to organize and print photos and ideas for showcasing souvenirs.

In Kerouac's *On the Road,* he wrote a simple line that found its way onto the bedroom wall of my adolescence, "The road must eventually lead to the whole world." I believed that then, and with greater strength I still believe that today. Our world is a beautiful complex beast. It's full of roads that lead to life's secrets; some shield themselves in shadow and are waiting to be discovered by young minds hungry for change and progress. Others are bright beacons welcoming you into the awaiting arms of a people, a place, and a culture that you never realized was home until you tasted the experience. Wherever your road leads, go with an open mind and eagerness to learn and empathize with the way life teems and tangles around you—open your heart to the people and places of this world.

I hope this book helps you find your road.

When we think back on our best road trips, we reflect on what we saw, what we ate, and what we experienced. Rarely do we think about how our adventures were made easier and worry-free by the way we planned our route or packed our bags. But when a trip goes badly, it can corrupt the desire to take to the road once more. There is something sort of wonderful about the idea of abandon, journeying far from home without a map or a planned route. In a sense, the notion of such fearless travel is what drew me to the road in the first place so many years ago. But taking the time to plan creates a solid foundation on which to build your adventure, especially when traveling with children.

Start by researching your destinations. Read reviews of hotels and restaurants, attractions and historical sites, and planned events in the area. Visit their websites and ensure the hours are cohesive with your schedule and any tourist site you may seek out is not closed for the season or under renovation. Once you've established your plans at each location, study the roads that will take you there. Look for scenic, safe back road alternatives and map out ways to access the interstate from those byways. With this outline of a plan, you'll find your preparation taking on a life of its own. Then turn to the tips in this section to ensure your car is ready for the road and that you pack (and snack) efficiently and wisely.

PLANNING AND CAR READINESS

ARE YOU READY TO HIT THE ROAD? As exciting as the prospect of jumping in your car and taking off this minute may be, being mindful of a few simple steps before you take to the road will ensure a safe and much more enjoyable journey.

PLANNING YOUR TRIP

It may seem obvious, but plan a route—every single step. Where you're staying, where you want to eat, things you want to see. As long as you have a plan, it's easy to deviate. I am a meticulous planner and I always create a travel packet for the car. After securing all of our hotel or campsite reservations, I print and staple them together in chronological order in two sets—outbound travel and inbound travel. By doing this, I have all the addresses, phone numbers, and pertinent dates at my fingertips.

I also make notes on the back of each paper about restaurants and noteworthy sites. There are a couple of wonderful websites and apps that I've noted in the reference section that specialize in road food. You can search by city and state as well as type of cuisine. We will occasionally hone in on diners that have been featured on Food Network or Travel Channel shows, or seek out certain travel and food publications "best of" lists to create our dining wish list. We've had hits and misses, but I've always been grateful that we had a plan.

But don't be afraid to get a little sidetracked. One of my favorite road trip pastimes is to follow the billboards. Nowhere is this more entertaining than traveling the highways and byways of the American Southwest. The roads are dotted with signs both big and small advertising everything from rattlesnake pits and three-headed calves to cowboy boots and moccasins. Isn't that what the great American road trip is about really, the adventure of it all? Don't be intimidated by side and back roads; these often lead to tiny towns off the beaten path.

READYING THE CAR

Aside from careful planning, the most important thing to do before your trip is to ensure your car is ready for the road. There are both benefits and downfalls to renting a car or driving your own vehicle. Renting a car is obviously an added expense. However, if your car is older and you have concerns about it making the journey safely, renting may be worth the extra cost. If something happens to your rental in the midst of your trip, you are covered by the company's roadside assistance and your contract. By driving your own car, you're putting extra mileage and wear and tear on your vehicle. That said, I love driving my own car and the "wear and tear," even from a jaunt across the country, will not offset the out-of-pocket expense to rent a vehicle for that length of time. The most important consideration is the condition of your car. Are the tires in good shape? Any oil leaks or other issues that have come to light during regular maintenance?

To ensure that you're covered in all sorts of situations, join a roadside assistance program. Most of the basic memberships will cover towing for the first 10 miles to the nearest service station. Premier memberships often include up to 100 towing miles and all for less than the cost of an average tow. Some assistance programs such as AAA also offer free TripTiks (marked and mapped plans of your trip), discounts at hotels, restaurants, attractions, and more.

Here are lists of the most important things to have checked out before hitting the road.

ASK YOUR
FAVORITE
TRUSTED
MECHANIC
TO

+ Check the tread on your tires

+ Check your tire pressure

+ Ensure your spare tire is in good shape

+ Check that all connections and hoses are in good shape and tight

+ Replace all dead fuses

+ Check your oil level and ensure there are no leaks

+ Check the life of your battery

+ Check the car's coolant level

+ Address any major repair concerns

OTHER CAR-RELATED REMINDERS BEFORE YOU HEAD OUT

+ Program your GPS

+ Bring paper maps that cover your route in case you lose your GPS signal

+ Ensure your registration and insurance are in the car

+ Clear out any trash or items that are not needed

+ Clean your car inside and out—it feels good to start a road trip in a clean car

+ Place an extra key/key fob in your wallet in case of emergency

+ Prep your iPod or CD changer with your selected road music and/or podcasts

+ Place all charging wires and associated plugs in a Ziploc in your glove compartment for easy access

As important as it is to be prepared, allow time for spontaneity. Just be sure to have a near-full tank of gas and venture off earlier in the day to avoid getting caught somewhere in the dark. It's hard to believe that in this age there are still pockets of the world that don't provide strong cellular coverage—but they are often the most beautiful. By adventuring during daylight hours, you'll stay safer and have the important ability to best read a proper paper road map. The extra care you put into planning your travels will be rewarded with the peace of mind that if trouble waits on the road, you are prepared to handle the situation efficiently and safely.

2

—

ORGANIZATION
AND PACKING

WHETHER YOU'RE HEADING OUT for a weekend or a month on the road, organizing your car and bags will make a world of difference. If you do a lot of traveling on the road, creating go-to packing lists makes the task relatively painless. I have lists for overnight travels and weekend road trips, and lists that cover longer journeys as well. It's okay to deviate from these master lists, but having the basics covered helps in two ways: it ensures that you have everything packed and ready to go and that nothing is forgotten; and, conversely, you can review the checklist when you're packing up to head home, so you can avoid leaving any favorite clothes or toys behind.

Here are some basic lists to get you started. You can alter the lists based on your needs, lifestyle, and time of year in which you are traveling; obviously what you need for a camping trip will differ from that of a quick jaunt to the city. I have started with a list for an overnight trip, and each list builds on that foundation. Having spent the last twenty years traveling roads the world over, I have also learned to travel lightly—this most assuredly takes some patience and confidence. The need or desire

THE OVERNIGHT TRIP	THE WEEKEND TRIP
As for any type of travel, your destination will strongly dictate what you pack. This list covers the absolute basics; you can add additional pieces as needed.	2 t-shirts/tops 1 button-down 1 pair of jeans/pants (2 for men) 1 pair of leggings (for women) 1 sweater 1 jacket 2 pairs of socks 3 pairs of underwear 1 bathing suit 1 or 2 pairs of shoes 1 hat Laundry bag to collect dirty clothes
1 t-shirt/top 1 button-down (I love chambray or denim shirts) 1 pair of jeans/pants 1 sweater 1 jacket 1 pair of socks 1 pair of underwear 1 nightgown or tee for sleeping 1 bathing suit 1 or 2 pairs of shoes 1 hat Laundry bag to collect dirty clothes	

to overpack will obviously depend on where you are going and what you are doing, but be critical and a ruthless editor—especially when bringing your family along; schlepping all that luggage in and out of the car every night really can be avoided.

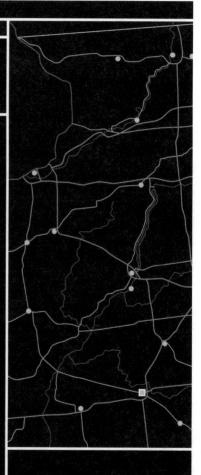

THE TWO-WEEK ROAD TRIP

On a trip this long, we usually make at least one laundry stop and we always limit ourselves to one bag per person, plus a small personal bag (for books, sketchbook, iPod, etc.). If you have younger children, try to pack all the kids clothes together to save space.

....

3 to 5 t-shirts/tops
2 button-downs
1 pair of jeans/pants (2 for men)
1 pair of leggings (for women)
1 sweater
1 jacket
7 pairs of socks
7 pairs of underwear
1 bathing suit
1 pair of sandals or flip-flops
1 pair of sneakers
1 pair of boots ▶

1 hat
Laundry bag to collect dirty
    clothes

The best tip ever for packing clothing efficiently is based on a little trick I learned in Navy boot camp. In order for us to get all of our uniform requirements into one Navy-issued seabag, we learned to roll. Fold your clothing lengthwise, roll tightly, and place in your bag. Fill airholes with undies and socks—you will be amazed by how much you can fit in your luggage.

ADDITIONAL PACKING LISTS

Aside from clothing, you'll likely pack your toiletries and electronic and personal items. The lists provided here cover both necessities and extras.

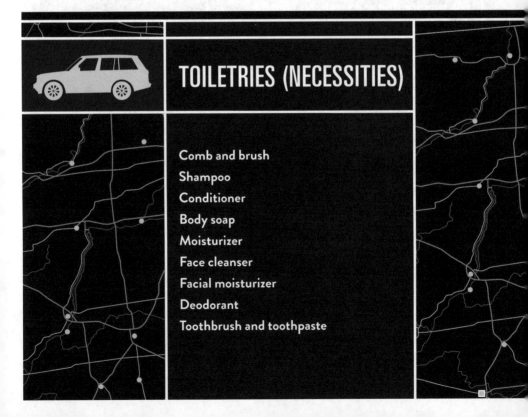

TOILETRIES (NECESSITIES)

Comb and brush
Shampoo
Conditioner
Body soap
Moisturizer
Face cleanser
Facial moisturizer
Deodorant
Toothbrush and toothpaste

TOILETRIES (EXTRAS TO CONSIDER)

Makeup and travel brushes
Hair care products
Contacts and solution
Eye drops
Tweezers
Nail clippers
Q-tips
Cotton wipes

ADDITIONAL ITEMS FOR KIDS

Modify this list based on your children's ages as this one focuses primarily on infants and toddlers. For the sake of avoiding repetition, the other clothing and toiletries lists apply to children as well; simply alter those lists based on your needs.

Diapers
Diaper cream
Changing mat
(continued on next page ▶)

Wipes
Feeding bibs
Burp cloths
Plastic spoon and fork
Baby food
Breast pump (if needed)
Formula (if needed)
Sippy cups
Portable potty
Small plastic bucket (in case of car sickness)
Thermometer
Booster or portable high chair
Portable crib or bassinet
Night-light
Stroller

UTILITIES/ELECTRONICS

Auto essentials (oil, spare, tire gage, jumper cables, rags, duct tape)
GPS
Real maps or road atlas
Camera

Chargers and extra batteries
Flashlight
Battery booster
Spare keys
Coins for tolls
First-aid kit for car (see following list)
A smaller first-aid kit for stops (restaurants, hikes, playgrounds, etc.)
Any medication you take, plus: Pepto-Bismol and/or antacids (for upset stomach), Tylenol (for mild pain and headaches), Benadryl (for mild allergies), Arnica (to soothe sore muscles and bruises), and Rescue Remedy (to keep calm and carry on)
Bug spray
Sunscreen
Sunglasses
Hand sanitizer
Ziplocs (for wet swimsuits, or to gather trash between stops)
Paper towels (for car cleanups)
Toilet paper (you never know (continued on next page ▶)

when you'll be on a long stretch of road
with no options)
Rain gear (disposable ponchos have saved
us more than once!)
Umbrella (compact, collapsible are the
most travel-friendly)
Collapsible tote bags
Printed confirmations
Blankets and pillows for car

FIRST-AID KIT

Band-Aids (varying sizes)
Antiseptic cream (like Neosporin)
Rolled bandages
Sticky tape
Roll-on anti-itch cream (for bug bites and
mild rashes)
Disposable gloves
Alcohol-free wipes
Scissors
Tweezers
Safety pins

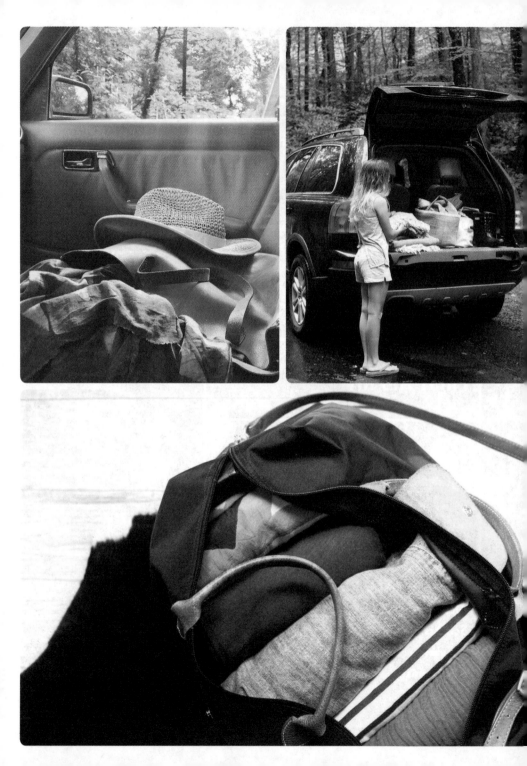

 PACKING FOR KIDS

Preparing your bags and vehicle for traveling safely and relatively pain-free with children just takes a bit of planning. We've covered packing their necessities in the last few pages. Just ensure that everything that provides them with entertainment in the car is reachable for them, and anything you may need to be in charge of (wipes, snacks, bottles, etc.) is reachable for you. Every child is unique in what keeps their little hands and minds occupied, so apart from the following suggestions, be mindful of your own children and what they love and loathe.

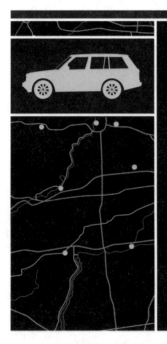

+ Create a small pack of DVDs if you have the means to play them. Try to include something they have not seen before to help hold their interest.

+ Create activity packs for each child. Great items for the car include coloring books, colored pencils (avoid markers—trust me), loose paper, notebooks, favorite books, and lap games such as road bingo. Store these items in the door pocket or chair pockets (continued on next page ▶)

for easy access. Kids should be able to reach everything they need without unbuckling their seatbelts.

+ New books and small toys provide a wonderful distraction from the impatience kids will often suffer in the back seat. I always surprise the kids with a new book on the way out of town and a little something as we head home. Be mindful when considering what toys to bring in the car—you don't want to be digging for lost Legos at every rest stop.

+ Create snack packs. You can create smaller snack packs for each child for each day on the road or create a cache of snacks for the whole car. Ensure that the snacks are easy to open, non-choking hazards, and full of protein. (See chapter 3 for ideas.)

+ Each child should have a blanket and something to help them sleep—a lovey or a small familiar pillow that gives them the comfort of home.

+ If your car does not have tinted windows, consider purchasing inexpensive shades that stick to the inside of the passenger windows. Blinding sun can prevent a child who's ready to nap from falling asleep peacefully.

(continued on next page ▶)

+ Make pit stops. Often. I used to be able to power through a ten-hour drive with just one rest stop. Kids changed everything. After a sixteen-hour drive back to Omaha with a fourteen-month-old, I promised I would never put my daughter, or myself, through that nightmare again. Rest stops are important. Quick stops are necessary, but longer layovers will make your trip memorable as opposed to stressful. Resign yourself to the fact that it simply takes longer to travel with children and that's okay. Your little ones are inadvertently asking you to slow down and smell the proverbial roses. (See the resources for some ideas about how to make the most of your stops.) One of our favorite rest stops was the obscure little Superman Museum in Metropolis, Illinois. Be spontaneous and ready for adventure—and ready for the kids to help take the lead.

⦿ LOADING UP THE CAR

When packing your car, take a moment to think about where everyone in your family sits. Make things easy to access for your passengers as well as yourself. You shouldn't be fishing around for anything while driving! This mindful organization can also make unloading and reloading the car after each day easier.

SOME TIPS TO KEEP IN MIND

+ If you have three overnights in a row, then a week at your destination, pack smaller bags to tote into the hotel each night so you don't have to unload the entire trunk. This takes some careful planning and attention to detail—and I've had to go back out to the car and dig something out of our bigger bags more than once—but it can make your life much easier.

+ Roll outfits together for the kids and Ziploc each separately with their name and day of the week—this totally beats unpacking everything every night at the hotel.

+ Be sure to organize the trunk of your car for easy unloading. Bury any larger items that you know you don't need until you reach your final destination. After a long day on the road, you don't want to stand in a hotel parking lot or campground unpacking and repacking your car every night.

(continued on next page ▶)

+ Create an area in your car (either a back passenger seat or your tailgate) that is prepped and ready to go for impromptu diaper changing. Keep a small stocked tote near that designated area, or at your feet, so you can clean up your child quickly without digging through larger bags.

....

+ Create an easily accessible bag to hold any charging devices and electronics (Kindles, iPads, etc.) and store in the glove compartment or center console.

....

+ Have a small tote ready to go for pit stops. This should include your small first-aid kit, sunglasses, bug spray, sunscreen, small books and toys (to help occupy children in restaurants), and any snacks and feeding utensils you may need.

3

—

ROAD SNACKS

THE TEMPTATION to stop at every roadside café is a major problem for me. What if they have the absolute best banana cream pie in the world and we just drove by without knowing?! Unfortunately, this has rubbed off on the children a bit as well. We love new discoveries on the road and, for us, the most exciting of those discoveries often involves food. But there are always long stretches of road that yield no promising gourmand memories, so it's always safe to have some snacks packed for easy access. Here are some ideas for keeping you and your travel buddies happily nibbling while on the road.

⊙ STORE-BOUGHT SNACKS

Taking a road trip is pretty awesome, and I love celebrating adventure. As such, traveling is one of the few times I make exceptions to what my children are allowed to eat. Here is a list of some of our favorite store-bought snacks for adults and kids alike. I tend to avoid anything too messy like large crackers, chips, anything with a dip or sauce, and of course anything that melts!

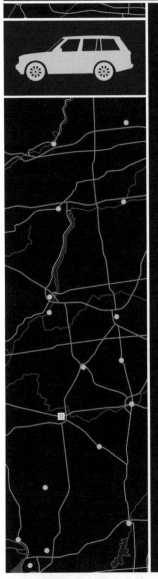

+ Lollipops! We love the organic lollipops from Trader Joe's. Sometimes you need a little quiet in the car and this is the perfect device for implementing a bit of peace. Somehow, they seem to magically make the time go a little faster as well.

+ Small, bite-size crackers are a favorite and (relatively) crumble-free. We love Annie's Organic Bunny Grahams as they come in a variety of flavors.

+ Apples, bananas, and clementine oranges are all great options for older kids; be sure to have a large Ziploc ready for peels and cores.

+ Fruit purees in a squeezable tube or pouch are great for both kids and adults and don't require refrigeration.

+ Cheese and meat sticks provide much needed protein and keep kids from asking when lunch is every five minutes.

+ Granola bars and protein bars are another protein-packed option.

+ My personal favorites include chocolate-covered raisins, Fig Newtons, and honey-roasted peanuts.

⦿ HOMEMADE TREATS

You can stock up on store-bought snacks, but I really love bringing home-baked goods along—it's a wonderful little reminder that home is just a highway away.

PEANUT BUTTER ENERGY BITES

This delicious no-bake recipe comes together quickly and is full of fiber, protein, and omega-3s. As a result, these bites really keep hunger at bay between meal stops. Be careful, they disappear quickly if you don't mind the container!

MAKES 2 DOZEN

1 cup peanut butter

½ cup honey

1⅛ cup nonfat dry milk

1 cup oatmeal, toasted

1 teaspoon buckwheat, uncooked

1 teaspoon millet, uncooked

1 tablespoon red and white quinoa, uncooked

½ cup chocolate chips, chopped roughly

1. Using a stand or hand-mixer, combine the peanut butter, honey, and dry milk until fully incorporated.

2. In another bowl mix the oatmeal, buckwheat, millet, quinoa, and chocolate chips together. Add this to the peanut butter mixture and beat until the ingredients are thoroughly combined. Using your hands, shape the dough into small, 1-inch balls.

3. Place the balls in the fridge to set up for a few hours, or enjoy them soft and tasting like cookie dough. Store in an airtight container or Ziploc for up to a week.

HELEN'S REUBEN BAKE

My recollections of taking road trips across the Southwest are punctuated with the memory of my grandmother Helen's Reuben Bake. Usually made at the boisterous request of my brother and I, this savory snack was not necessarily road food. But she always made a lot . . . and there were always leftovers. Wrapped in tinfoil and kept in a small cooler, this was the best midday treat in the back seat.

MAKES ONE LOAF (ABOUT 12 SLICES)

1 (store-bought) pizza crust

3 tablespoons Thousand Island dressing

8–10 ounces corned beef, thinly sliced

½ cup sauerkraut, drained (optional; I make it without for my kids)

4 ounces swiss cheese, shredded or thinly sliced

Egg wash (1 egg whisked with 2 tablespoons water)

Caraway seeds

1. Preheat the oven to 375°F. Prepare a large baking sheet with a light mist of nonstick cooking spray. Transfer your dough to the baking sheet and, using a rolling pin or your hands, shape the dough into a long oval.

2. Spread the dressing down the middle of the dough, leaving about 2 inches free of dressing on both sides down the length of the dough. Layer the corned beef on top of the dressing, then add the sauerkraut, if using. Top with the cheese.

3. With a paring knife make diagonal cuts about 1 inch apart down each

side of the dough. Be careful not to start your cuts too close to the filling. Then working from one side to the next, fold the strips of dough on top of each other to enclose the filling inside the dough (you can pull them a bit as needed as the dough is fairly elastic). Brush the top of the dough very lightly with the egg wash and sprinkle with the caraway seeds.

4. Bake for 20 minutes or until the top begins to turn light gold and you can see the cheese bubbling through the holes in the dough. Let cool for about 15 minutes before slicing. To pack for the road, be sure to cool each slice completely, wrap the pieces separately in tinfoil and store in a small cooler.

APPLE MOONS

The kids love snacking on these little cookies. Based on my favorite rugelach recipe, these little gems work beautifully as a make-ahead snack and won't get icky when left in a warm car once in a while—if they last that long. Feel free to experiment with different fillings (see my list for additional ideas).

MAKES ABOUT 3 DOZEN COOKIES

1 cup butter, softened

3 tablespoons sugar plus 1 tablespoon for sprinkling

⅛ teaspoon salt

8 ounces cream cheese

1 egg yolk (save the white)

1 teaspoon almond extract

2 cups flour

FOR THE FILLING

¼ cup apple butter

¼ cup chopped almonds or almond slivers, lightly toasted

3 tablespoons sugar combined with 1 teaspoon cinnamon

Egg wash (leftover egg white whisked with 2 tablespoons water)

1. To make the dough, combine the butter, sugar, and salt in a mixing bowl and beat until light and fluffy. Add the cream cheese, egg yolk, and almond extract, and beat until fully incorporated. Slowly add the flour and mix until fully combined. Scrape the bowl if needed and beat for one more minute.

2. Divide the dough into two equally sized discs and wrap them separately with plastic wrap. Place the dough in the fridge for at least one hour.

3. When the dough is ready, preheat the oven to 350°F and prepare a large baking sheet with a light coating of nonstick spray and a piece of parchment paper cut to fit your baking sheet.

4. Flour a work surface and roll out one of the discs into a flat round shape about 12 inches across. Top with the apple butter, spreading it evenly and leaving about a ½-inch border of dough exposed around the perimeter. Add the almonds and sprinkle with the cinnamon sugar mixture.

5. Using a knife or pizza cutter cut the dough into 16 wedges, as you would slice a pizza. One at a time, starting from the outside, roll each piece inward to create a croissant-like shape. Place each cookie on the baking sheet and turn the ends in slightly to make the shape of

a crescent moon. Repeat this process with the second disc of dough. Brush the cookies lightly with egg wash and sprinkle with sugar. Bake at 350°F for 25 minutes or until the cookies begin to turn golden and the filling begins to bubble. Once cooled, store in an airtight container for up to a week.

SOME IDEAS FOR FILLING VARIATIONS

+ Strawberry or blueberry jam with a sprinkle of chocolate chips
+ Lemon curd and walnuts
+ Orange marmalade and pecans
+ Raspberry jam and white chocolate chips
+ Cinnamon sugar and drizzles of honey
+ Light wash of melted butter, cinnamon sugar, raisins, and chopped walnuts

Whether you create a host of home-baked goods to pack on your road trip or raid your local grocery store before heading out of town, just be sure to keep food handy. This is especially important with children in tow. Allowing them to lightly graze between meals equals happy and sated bellies; and parents know, happy bellies means happy kids. Likewise, be open to trying restaurants outside your normal comfort zone when traveling. You may be pleasantly surprised, and of course this means you're fully embracing the idea that the road leads to adventure, all sorts.

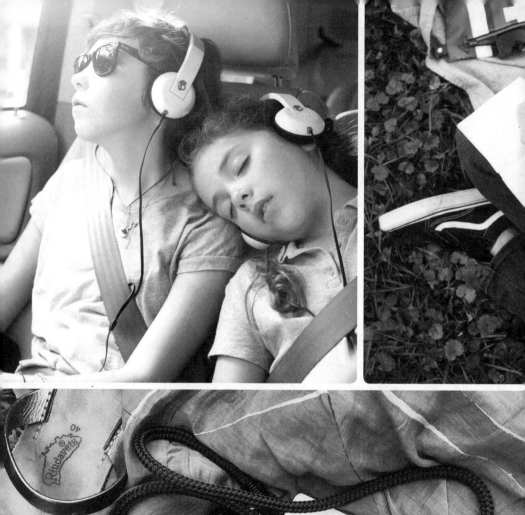

PART TWO THE TRAVEL RECORD

As individuals, we all see the world through a lens of our own experience, impressions, and personal aesthetics. In a digital world that revolves around social media and the vast resources of images that live online, it can be a challenge to take back our own vision. More than any other personal experience, travel grants you the opportunity to see the world on your own terms rather than others' curated views. What you take from that experience and visual journey is just as important as your initial decision to get behind the wheel and drive into your proverbial sunset in the first place. It is important to record your travels, and it is important to do this for you and you alone. Whether you prefer a visual way of recording your travels through photographing or sketching, or perhaps marrying pen to paper, remember that this is for *you*. Your mission is not to share these stories and ideas on social media—it's a quiet, introspective creative process that allows you to explore your surroundings deeply, to truly observe in a way you may have never experienced. Of course you may share your work with anyone you choose, but beginning this process with that in mind can easily corrupt your vision and the outcome of your story.

This section covers three ways of creating a travel record: visual storytelling, travel journals, and mixtapes. I encourage you to explore each chapter without trying to choose one method over another. Rather, each way of observing the world and recording your findings is incredibly personal; as such, these concepts are meant to blend and overlap within your process to create tangible evidence of experiencing something that you never want to forget.

4

—

VISUAL
STORYTELLING

MOST TRAVELERS always seem to have a camera in hand, prepared to shoot everything they come across. I can appreciate this way of recording your travels. There is a sense of urgency to it—when will you return, when will this moment ever happen again? But powerful imagery, photographs that stir your soul and sweep you into their arms with the sweet lullaby of memory, require a moment of reflection. While social media has changed how we exchange information, and tech-savvy road trippers are now shooting and sharing as they go, more intentional photos result in sacred moments of creation that tell a visual story. Rather than returning from your trip with hundreds of images that just sit on your hard drive or your phone, imagine for a moment that they could live on. In this section, we'll talk about how to construct a visual story from your travel images and cover some basics about traveling with your camera so you can get the most out of your photography.

TELLING A STORY

How do we tell a story? Our most ancient form of storytelling is an oral tradition. But as technology has evolved with our desire to communicate creatively, visuals have become equally imperative to the tale. A story can be told by one powerful photograph or, more traditionally, by a collection of frames, each moving the story forward. Just like written tales, focus on creating an introduction, elaboration, climax, and conclusion to your story. Most visual storytellers begin with a wide-framed shot to set the stage, then a medium range to set a more intimate atmosphere; the next is usually a detail shot, then a portrait to capture the emotion of your subject, then action. The first image should be especially powerful. While this image order is common, it does not have to be followed. This diversity of framing creates your sense of pacing, giving each shot a moment to breathe before the next. Remember that each picture should have a purpose and move the story forward; pictures should not be redundant. And editing is so important. Take personal relationships with certain shots out of the editing process—use only images that move the story along.

The more you start to capture your travel images this way, the more mindful you will become of the story as a whole and what you wish to share. Remember, while traveling you are not setting the stage for your story, it is unfolding before you. It is your responsibility to recognize that story and capture the frames in a way that make sense to you. Here are some other aspects to consider when using photography to tell your travel story.

COMPOSITION

In the realm of photography, the art of composition is the most important factor in sharing your story. While your camera's capabilities will understandably dictate many facets of your picture-taking, composition is the one aspect controlled entirely by you. What you choose to shoot and how you choose to shoot it are how you'll create a style of recording your travels that is inherently all your own. Recognizing a strong composition is an intuitive skill and the result of keenly observing the world around you. As you practice visualizing objects, people, and light with your photographer's eye, you'll start noticing compositions wherever you go. As the photographer, you are so much more than the person who takes the photograph—you're also the curator and the storyteller.

Most of us consider framing to be the edges or borders of our image, much like a wooden picture frame upon your desk. But a frame is more than the edge of the photograph. Framing is an essential key to visual storytelling and can be a powerful element when creating a sense of place within your images. Push your comfort zone and look at this compositional element anew. Consider including frames *within* your frame, lines and shapes that edge your subject and draw the eye deeper into the photo to set a sense of place and emotion: the branches of a tree, the lines of a building, a window, or even a door frame. For example, perhaps you've pulled over to a dusty roadside café to take a break from your drive. Your friend has taken a seat across from you in the booth, and the way the sun is coming in through the window illuminates her beautifully. You could shoot her close up with magical light blanketing her form, creating a warm and welcoming scene. However, if you were to step back through the restaurant, using the partly closed glass door of the entrance as your frame, the story suddenly becomes far more intimate, the viewer now looking in on this woman who's making her way through the world. Think of framing as movie stills. It adds to your photograph a layer of curiosity, wonder, and a desire to know more.

LIGHT

Light is where the magic sleeps. Apart from composition, it is the most important element to consider when taking a photograph, and once you learn to really and truly *see* light, to make it bend to your wishes and desires, then you become a part of that magic. Many people who photograph casually, shooting simply to record moments, may be surprised to learn that direct, midday sun is not necessarily the best light to capture your travels. That's not to say don't shoot that time of day, just be mindful about *what* you're shooting during those hours. Midday, or full-sun, can create harsh and unflattering shadows and there is little visual warmth to this type of light. However, it is ideal for wide shots of landscapes and cityscapes. For portraits, shaded areas during this time of day

will vary, but try to find light shade—something that is evenly shaded—and the resulting photograph will be much more flattering. Ideally, the best time of day to photograph portraits is in the morning or the evening. The light is soft and incredibly flattering to whatever you are photographing. When you see the beautiful tones in your images, you will understand why this type of light is commonly referred to as "the golden hour." Another lighting situation you are sure to encounter outside is cloud cover. Do not let this discourage you. Cloud cover provides a soft, even light that can be beautiful in portraits and still lifes.

CAMERAS

You do not have to own the most state-of-the-art camera and lenses to create beautiful imagery from your road trips. You are not on assignment; you are not under any pressure to document aside from what you put on yourself. When my husband and I traveled to Pawleys Island (a story you'll find in part 3), I brought only my phone to capture our travels. It was so important that we really respected our time together, and lugging all my cameras along would have made it feel more like work than vacation. I have friends who travel with as many as five cameras, and others who now solely rely on their smartphones. Do what feels right to you. While it's important to document and record, remember that it's about the expedition. Do not get so tied up in your desire to tell a story and share your images that you forget to live and breathe, feel and consume every experience the road beckons you to taste.

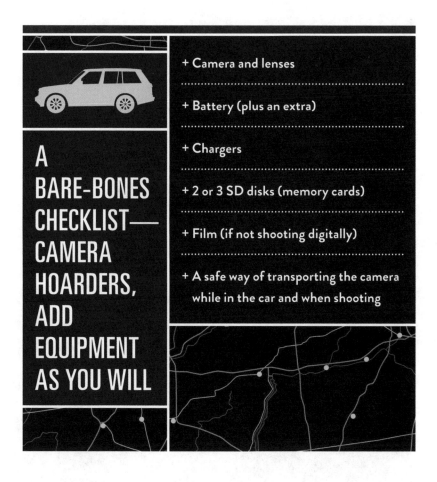

A BARE-BONES CHECKLIST— CAMERA HOARDERS, ADD EQUIPMENT AS YOU WILL

+ Camera and lenses

+ Battery (plus an extra)

+ Chargers

+ 2 or 3 SD disks (memory cards)

+ Film (if not shooting digitally)

+ A safe way of transporting the camera while in the car and when shooting

Road trips are my favorite excuse to bring my instant cameras along on a journey, and the resulting images give you the instant gratification of creating something tangible. An extra bonus? They are the perfect element to highlight places and certain events in your travel journal. They are also an excellent

means of getting kids involved in recording your trip. Our kids love their Fuji Instax cameras, and it was our daughter Aela who first started taping her shots into her travel book when she was just eight years old and writing about what she photographed.

5

TRAVEL
JOURNALS

WHEN I WAS FOURTEEN, my mother gave me a copy of Julia Cameron's *The Artist's Way*. At the time, she was a devotee of Morning Pages, a writing device conceptualized in the book that prompts you to write a number of pages every morning, regardless of whether you have anything to say or not. It is believed that a forced writing schedule, or flow writing, can open up a part of your mind allowing for open consciousness—almost a type of meditation. My mother wanted me to experience the same sort of enlightenment that she had discovered through her morning practice.

I have always struggled with journaling. I would continue to purchase beautiful new journals—their blank, empty pages teasing me with their hollowness, daring me to mark them and make them my own. There can be a level of intimidation when it comes to journaling. I would begin a journal every year with the purest of intentions to see those pages through until the end of the year; I don't think I ever got past February.

I found that I was only truly compelled to journal when I was traveling, and that my style of journaling was bulleting my daily events, almost like taking field notes. Frequently I was inspired to embellish this language, and often those entries read more like a diary of a sixteenth-century maiden (I was the high school girl reading Shakespeare in her free time). As my travel journaling became more natural, I began to sketch, slip papers into my book, and add songs and funny stories that occurred along the way.

The first rule about keeping a travel journal is to record. And that is the only rule. Whether you decide to do so through words, sketches, and collected papers, find what feels natural, not forced. When you do, you'll find peace and reprise from reaching for your journal, not a trepidation about what to say or do. Grace Coddington, the creative director of American *Vogue* magazine, once said that she never sleeps or works when on the train or in a taxi, whether that city be new to her or not. She doesn't want to miss anything, "Always keep your eyes open. Keep watching. Because whatever you see can inspire you." The beauty of travel journaling is that it demands that you take a moment to quiet your mind and truly focus on your experiences and how you're reacting to this new world unfolding around you. Don't be afraid to only focus on your passion—if your primary focus of traveling is tasting the world, picking apart delicious food on your travels, and taking copious notes, the result can lead to successfully recreating those flavors at home.

Several of my friends share their journals with us on the next few pages. Each is a distinctly different style to illustrate that there is truly no wrong way to keep a travel journal. I want you to be inspired by their diversity of use and moved to start your own journal the next time you take to the open road.

Q&A LISA CONGDON

I first came across Lisa Congdon's illustrations through a mutual business acquaintance. I fell in love with not only Lisa's modernism meets whimsy drawings, but who she is as a human being. Over the years, I have found her to be a fierce advocate for so many issues close to my own heart, unyieldingly compassionate for everyone around her, and a selfless teacher and mentor to women entrepreneurs in particular. A few years ago, after returning from a trip to Portugal, she shared some shots of her sketchbooks. They were like nothing I had ever seen: just a word or two paired with full-page illustrations. They moved my heart. Lisa helped alter my perceptions of what journaling was meant to be, and I am forever grateful.

A BRIEF INTERVIEW WITH LISA CONGDON

Q: What inspires you to keep a travel journal?

A: I am an artist, and my greatest inspiration for my work comes from traveling. Keeping a travel journal helps me to capture what I'm seeing in a way that photographs can't. Taking photos is also super important to me, but my travel journals help me to have a more tactile experience in the moment and in the actual place—a way to capture the sights, the smells, the colors, the cultural symbols, and the ephemera I collect (ticket stubs, pieces of paper or packaging, that kind of thing). It's also a way for me to communicate what I'm seeing in my own voice to the people who follow and consume my work. And, ultimately, what I keep there sometimes leads to new work back in my studio at home—new themes, new colors, patterns, and landscapes.

Q: What do you keep in your journaling kit? Tell us about your process.

A: Generally I carry with me a small, compact travel watercolor case, a variety of pens, a handful of colored pencils and erasers, a little tape or glue for scrapbook pages, and, of course, a journal! All of these things go into a larger pouch. I end up carrying a lot of art supplies around with me, but it's totally worth it.

Q: Has your style of journaling changed over the course of your travels?

A: I made my first ever travel journal way back in 2003 before I was a professional artist. I was just starting to draw and paint when I went to Thailand for a month. Every single day I sat down to fill pages with pictures and writing about what I was doing and experiencing. At the time, the writing was the predominant feature in my travel journals, with some collages of ephemera I collected and maybe a handful of drawings. Today, it's the reverse! Drawing is my new language and so most of my journals are filled mostly with pictures and very few words. I communicate almost entirely visually now.

Do you remember when Flickr was the old Instagram? I feel so lucky to have been a part of that early photography community. It was through a Polaroid project I created called *For the Love of Light* that I first came across Ann-Kathrin's work. There is a sense of tangible realism in everything she shoots—and she shoots film. All film. In today's digitized world, those true artists of the medium are becoming incredibly rare. She is a light-wrangling master and is known for her breathtaking portrait work. Ann-Kathrin has grown into an internationally acclaimed wedding photographer and travels the world over. Her journals reflect her unquenchable desire to truly live the fullest of international lives and celebrate moments both quiet and out loud.

A BRIEF INTERVIEW WITH ANN-KATHRIN KOCH

Q: What inspires you to keep a travel journal?

A: When I travel, I feel most like myself, free of the daily responsibilities and open to everything new. There is so much going on in my head. All the new sights and smells. I want to capture these adventures in a way that keeps the memories alive, capture my feelings at that exact point in time. This can be anything I see or feel. Sometimes it's just a small little moment that made me happy, like the clouds drifting over an endless landscape out my plane window or the smell of the plants early in the morning while I can hear waves crashing on the shore. By writing my thoughts down while I'm in the moment and capturing what I see in a photo I can process everything and preserve it as a long-lasting memory.

Q: What do you keep in your journaling kit? Tell us about your process.

A: I'm a photographer, so the most natural way for me to capture anything is to take a picture. If I have it with me, it's my Hasselblad camera. If not, it's my iPhone. I then take any downtime I have to write about what the last day felt like. This is usually early in the morning over coffee when my thoughts are fresh or on a plane, high above the clouds. I concentrate on the impressions and emotions that went with whatever I experienced. For the writing I use hotel stationery. There's always a little notepad. I like how uncomplicated it is to just write thoughts down

on it. I also like to take any mementos that work
on a visual level, like menus and maps. This
to me is the perfect combination of words and
images.

Q: Has your style of journaling changed over the
course of your travels?

A: I've only started this year as I was traveling a
lot for an extended time. I usually travel on my
own, so writing and photographing what I'm
seeing helps me process it all. I've really enjoyed
it as it makes me so much more aware of everything around me while I'm there. And then I get
to relive it again afterward when I go through
my notes and pictures and put them together.

Q&A HEIDI SWANSON

James Beard award–winning cookbook author and photographer, Heidi Swanson once bought a Polaroid of mine when I had
a print shop on Etsy. Her highly acclaimed blog, *101 Cookbooks*,
was already on my radar, and I remember how honored and ri-
diculously excited I felt when I saw her name on my list of or-
ders that day. She humbled me all over again by attending my
first instant photography workshop in Marrakech a number of

years ago. It was on that trip, sitting poolside in a grove of lemon trees, that she asked me a pretty simple question, "If you could write any book, what would it be about?" That was truly the day the idea for this book was born, and I have Heidi to thank for pulling out that quiet desire.

A BRIEF INTERVIEW WITH HEIDI SWANSON

Q: What inspires you to keep a travel journal?

A: It's a bit hazy, but I think I started writing notes in a little booklet to keep track of expenses. One of the first trips I remember doing this was to Italy. Wayne and I were young, broke, and traveling for weeks on extremely limited budgets. He might pay for a *pensione* one night, I would cover breakfast and lunch the next day, and perhaps train tickets. Keeping a list was an easy way to keep track of who was paying for what. I liked looking back on those lists, and remembering all of the places we'd visited together, and on future trips I started to make more specific daily notes about where we were and what I was seeing. The expense lists were relatively short lived. I refer to my journals often for recipe inspiration or to remember

some of the details and minutiae of places I've
visited.

Q: What do you keep in your journaling kit? Tell us
about your process.

A: I try to travel light. A small, lined Moleskin notebook and a pen or pencil. Tape.

Q: Has your style of journaling changed over the
course of your travels?

A: It evolves. Now, I tend to make daily notes and
thread those pages with lists. Lists have titles
like: Kyoto Recipe Inspiration, Favorite Moments, Mexico City Market Ingredients, Things
I Ate in Thailand.

◉ JOURNALING SUPPLIES

Not sure where to start? A blank notebook is a great beginning. Aside from that, I've compiled a list of supplies that are light and easy to transport—so compact, in fact, that you can easily throw them into your backpack or purse. The size of your journal and the tools you select will obviously depend on how you choose to journal, but it might be fun to include a couple of items you wouldn't normally bring along. You may never realize how a moment or landscape will inspire you on the road. I've also included a list of ideas to get you over that initial intimidation of a blank book. When selecting your materials, make sure they all fit into a medium-size pencil case.

◉ GETTING STARTED

Here are some ideas, prompts, and tips to get you started on your travel journal.

WORDS

Don't fancy yourself a writer? You may be surprised. Travel can awaken long dormant prose. Start simply by recording the events of your day: what you saw on the road, the music playing on the radio, any interesting meals or pit stops. Think of these as your field notes. As you become more comfortable with daily writing while traveling, add poetry or song lyrics to your book. You can

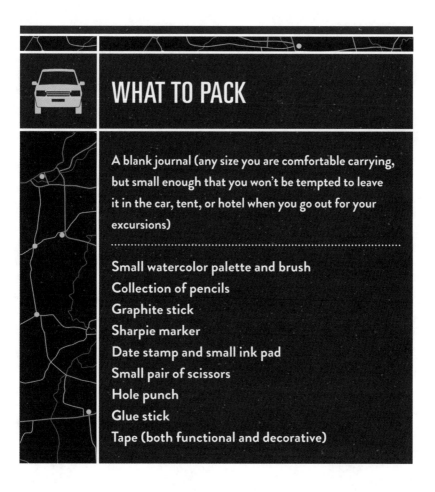

WHAT TO PACK

A blank journal (any size you are comfortable carrying, but small enough that you won't be tempted to leave it in the car, tent, or hotel when you go out for your excursions)

....

Small watercolor palette and brush
Collection of pencils
Graphite stick
Sharpie marker
Date stamp and small ink pad
Small pair of scissors
Hole punch
Glue stick
Tape (both functional and decorative)

quote something that you love that seems particularly relevant to what you are experiencing or you can craft your own prose with descriptive language. Travel asks us to step outside our norms and experience something new; carry this philosophy into how you record these fresh memories as well. As you record, you may find your story magically coming together. When I look back on my own notes, I find the small details that I never would have remembered otherwise are the memories that make me smile the most.

PHOTOS

If you travel with an instant camera like a Polaroid or an Instax, you can immediately add these quick snapshots to your book. Glue them in or use washi tape, draw around them or even on top of them—there are no rules!

DRAWING

As Lisa shared in her journal, some choose not to write at all but allow shape and line to tell their road stories. If you're not comfortable drawing, carry a small piece of graphite with you; rubbings can be an interesting way to add a visual component to your book. To make a rubbing, place a page of your journal on a surface and run the graphite over it until you capture the texture and shape of that object. Decorative tiles, architectural details, stones, and engraved bricks make wonderful rubbings.

COLLAGE

Collect paper, buy postcards, and save your receipts and dinner menus. Draw on them, write on them, and glue them into your book. While exploring journaling techniques for this book, I came across someone who was traveling across the United States and sending *themselves* a postcard at every stop. Upon their return home, they had a pile of cards that basically constituted a travel journal simply in need of binding.

FOR KIDS

I love Keri Smith's books. Buy your kids a copy of *Wreck This Journal* for your travels. Yes, there are plenty of road trip diaries specifically created for the younger crew, but I promise they won't enjoy them as much as they will this masterful little book. Each page is an adventure waiting to be had and a truly wonderful way for children to informally record their time on the road with you.

However you decide to structure your travel record, the most important thing is simply to keep one.

6

—

THE MIXTAPE

CERTAIN SONGS FILL THE AIR and carry you to the past. I truly fell in love with music at a very young age. It became a refuge from siblings, the poetry of my angst-ridden teenage heart, and anthems of uprise; it was my alarm clock in the morning and my lullaby at night. But nowhere was music selection more important to me than when I traveled. Like so many kids of the eighties, I created my first playlist by sleeping next to the stereo, waiting for my favorite songs to play on the radio so I could record them on my tape deck. I created a song list of what I wanted to capture and was hyper-diligent about ensuring I recorded each song in the order that I had pre-established. My Walkman was a constant companion on my family road trips, and there are still songs I hear today that transport me to those travels. Today, I continue to practice a thoughtful approach to my travel mixtapes. While they are constructed with digital files and a click of a button, I honor some of the same practices of my youth.

Playlists and mixtapes can easily permeate every aspect of your travels. You can prep playlists because you know you have many miles of road ahead and you're inspired by your ultimate destination. Or maybe you enjoy flipping through local stations as you move from town to town—certain songs will naturally stand out to you and your mixtape comes together while on the road. Jot these songs down in your travel journal and make a note about where you were or what you were doing when you heard it. When my best friend Amy and I traveled to Ireland, as you will read in the next section, I drove and she played DJ. She thoughtfully selected songs from her own iPod that represented not only the beauty of the land that surrounded us, the weather, and Ireland itself, but also songs that spoke to our friendship. It's one of my favorite playlists of all time, and every time I listen to it, Amy is beside me in soul and spirit.

Perhaps you and your best friend are bound for a road trip across Texas, seeking out the open spaces and beautiful solitude of a little town like Marfa. What do you think of when you visualize that trip? Americana and a little country perhaps? The beauty of digital music is that it's easy to access and download—if you have a theme in mind, start searching for musicians that fulfill the desired genre or mood. I have found some of my favorite artists this way. When I traveled to Iceland, I was already so in love with some of the artists from Scandinavia and the genre of Viking metal, I created a playlist to keep me company before arriving. Be open to seeking music out in every way you can imagine. While you may start a trip with a list of songs ready to go, you could find that you are adding to that list as the road leads you deeper into your travels.

A FEW ADDITIONAL POINTERS FOR CREATING A MEMORABLE MIXTAPE

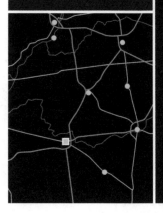

+ Listen to the way each song leads into the next. Does it flow or do you find the transitions jarring? Move songs around to ensure the changeovers complement each other.

+ Consider creating a story with your playlists if there are songs that chronologically tell the story of your travels (this is easiest to compose after the fact).

+ Don't be afraid to mix genres and musical styles—it's your mixtape; what it says to you is the most important.

+ If you have a favorite artist (or two, or three), absolutely add more than one song by each. Just ensure that you separate the songs out between other artists and choose tracks that vary from one another (example: a slower, then faster-paced song).

PART THREE   ROAD STORIES

In Keri Smith's *The Wander Society,* she writes, "We need more rambling, day-dreaming, thinking, perusing, being, looking, existing, allowing, ambling, opening, listening, because it teaches us what we are capable of. The nomadic tendency of wandering allows us to take pause, to consider what is really necessary, what is important for living well. In every moment of wandering, we experience awakening." To be fair, Smith's book encourages exploring your own surroundings, not necessarily setting out for a journey in which to discover these things. But so much of Smith's wandering manifesto can be studied as a means of gaining the most from your road travels as well.

In part 1, we discussed how important planning is when taking a road trip. So many factors go into not only creating the ideal route, but also deciding where to stay and how to pack for whatever may unfold. But there is a balance that we should all seek when traveling: a balance between preparedness and abandon. We must let the road lead us, not just the map or the guidebook. We must be open to adventure. We must be willing to let something else that's altogether unworldly guide our steps every so often.

These road stories are meant to inspire you. You'll note that each trip highlighted in this section reads like the pages from my journal; some will read more like field notes, some as descriptive narratives; the style of each is a reflection of how these trips resonated with me. The stories are divided by travel companion and speak to the unique circumstances that traveling by yourself or with friends or your partner—or your whole family—can present. Each story also features a small section at the end called "Bring It Home." It's not about the souvenirs; it's about what part of that trip you want to relive in your everyday life and how certain times and places enrich and inspire you.

7
—

SOLO TRIP //
THE DESERT

I LOVE TRAVELING ALONE. A lot of people aren't immediately comfortable with solo travel, but after several jaunts across Europe and Asia for work, I realized there was something beautiful and spiritual about being on the road by myself. Through traveling alone I've discovered more about who I am and how I see the world—what inspires me to create, to give, and to love not only as a human being, but as a wife, mother, daughter, and friend—than I have from most other experiences in my life. Embracing the solitude of the open road, succumbing to the magic of light and the depth of thoughts that dance across your mind as the miles fade behind you is personal evolution at its very best. For me, the places that hold the most sacred magic are the oldest. Find a place that whispers to your soul, a place where the earth vibrates with power beneath your feet, a place that feels like home though the comfort of your bed is miles away. There, you will discover yourself anew.

People have gathered in deserts for thousands of years to worship, cleanse, and practice self-care. The vast and hauntingly quiet places of the American Southwest easily lend themselves to solitude and reflection. Joshua Tree is full of hidden beauty—gold and platinum trees kiss the feet of the bald mountains and everywhere you turn is a cactus-encrusted rockscape. The light burns across the massive organic shapes that would love to call themselves little mountains—all shadow and brightness, hand in hand. These desert panoramas possess a stark, golden beauty—one that you must experience to truly appreciate. The desert's secret song asks to you look deeper, love harder, and take good care of yourself.

MY JOURNAL

I drove across California, from life to death to renewal. The sun was just beginning to dip behind the San Jacinto Mountains as I pulled my car into the small lot at Hope Springs Resort in Desert Hot Springs, California. A study in mid-century modernism meets minimalism, the modest hotel is situated in the cradle of the hills and overlooks the desert town below. As I was shown across the courtyard to my room, I could feel the warmth of the mineral springs lapping at my feet. I look to water to heal. I swim almost daily; it is my meditative time, where I can stretch my mind and body and be whole once more. The three pools that dotted the courtyard winked at me in the bright desert sun as if they knew my secret. Two French doors opened to a rather stark space. I found the king-size bed was on a platform on the floor and clad in a cloud of white bedding; the ground was concrete; the closet nonexistent. I was at first taken aback, but as I was left alone to unpack and settle in, I was grateful for the sparseness of the space. I came to reflect, to deepen my connection with the sacred places inside of me, and to relax. The room was perfect.

Joshua Tree was calling me, but I wasn't ready. I knew that once I entered the national park little else would hold my fascination over the next few days. So I set about exploring the area, including the small towns of Yucca Valley and of Joshua Tree itself. In these quiet hubs of activity I discovered antique and secondhand stores with labyrinths of curiosities, had my cards read for the first time in years, bought turquoise jewelry, and found what would become my favorite small-batch coffee from Joshua Tree Coffee Company. And I drove. I drove in silence—the sound of tires rolling beneath me, reminding me that

I'm searching for something—into Palm Springs and down the mother road of mid-century design with tourists worshipping at the altar of retail modernism. I drove past acres and acres of wind farms, so alien against the stark desert. I drove down the quiet roads of Twentynine Palms (where I stopped for a bear claw the size of my forearm) and skirted the border of the national forest all the way down to Cactus City and back up to Pioneertown.

Built in the 1940s as an Old West movie set, Pioneertown is a strange and wonderful place; more than fifty western-themed television shows and movies were filmed on "Mane" Street. The dirt road that leads between the buildings is still home to movie props and hitching posts. A few of the buildings are now inhabited by local artisans and serve as small studios and shops. But the reason I climbed the winding hill to Pioneertown was because of Pappy and Harriet's. Known for their barbeque and live music, it was the one place that countless friends told me not to miss. And I'm so happy I listened. While I sat at a small table looking out into the desert, the sun sank and the moon began to rise. I ate an enormous plate of ribs, drank a cold beer, and watched as the place filled with tourists, bikers, and young Los Angeles weekenders. As I left, the sky was painted in a wash of dusty pastels and the air bit my cheeks—all at once I craved the mineral springs.

I returned to the hotel that evening full of wonder. The warmth of the mineral springs was spiritually cleansing and enveloping. I moved back and forth from the refreshing lap spring to the full, rolling heat of the soaking tubs—all while spying a full moon that seemed to have swallowed the stars. One of the things I had looked forward to the most on this trip was seeing the desert night sky. But the glowing moon had other ideas, and I am grateful for its illumination.

I slept in. When traveling alone, there is very little accountability for where to be and when to be there. I took full advantage of this, reminding myself that while traveling alone is about discovery, self-care and reflection are of equal importance. The wide quiet spaces—the morning hush of the hotel room, a roadside vista view—whispered to me. They are why I came out here alone: to listen to the world, to listen to my heart. I was sure to take the time in bed to feel grateful for what I was experiencing and to look with unhurried anticipation to the day ahead of me. I lingered over breakfast, I sat poolside, reading the *New York Times*, drinking my coffee, and wondering what hidden magic I would find in the desert that day.

Upon finally crossing into Joshua Tree National Park, I felt something shift inside of me. It is an acute sensation that I've experienced before—as if crossing from one plane into another. National parks seem to hold that kind of energy. I didn't get very far down the road before I was compelled to pull over and shoot the landscape. That was the reoccurring theme of the day. How many photographs did I really need of these yucca trees? I wasn't in any state to answer that question at the time—each formation seemed an individual, unique, living sculpture and I had never seen anything like it before—I was enchanted. Listen. Listen to the way you are emotionally and physically responding to what you are seeing. Your creative mind will begin to process a new environment in ways you cannot fathom. But only if you listen carefully.

Walk. I hiked through one section of the park, discovered cave paintings, and just kept shooting. And I may have lost my way. There is a wonderful, albeit oft-overused quote, taken from J.R.R. Tolkien's *Fellowship of the Ring*: "Not all those who wander are lost." It simply means that we all wander with purpose.

Every journey somehow affects the way we view the world, or our place within it. I used to be worried to step off the proverbial trail; now, I sense there is always magic veiled in the hidden places. If we are fearless and curious enough to seek out that alchemy, we are forever changed. I found a deeply buried part of myself in the desert and I found that I didn't want to leave. I wanted to stay forever. As I drove out of the park and made my way back to Desert Hot Springs, I envisioned myself living here and my heart sang. I just wanted to soak in the springs and clear the desert dust from my mind and body.

The next morning, I packed my bag, said a sweet and almost tearful goodbye to that small, perfect hotel, and drove into Palm Springs. I checked into the Ace Hotel and sat in front of the fire just outside my room, staring into the flames and feeling so grateful for what I had experienced on the road. It was my last night in the desert, and I treated myself to dinner at Norma's at the achingly beautiful and elegant Parker Hotel. I sat on the porch alone, the sky darkening and the strung lights brightening, giggles of friends and couples coming from the labyrinth of greenery to my right. I ordered Claws n' Chips Gone Fishing, lobster served fish-and-chips style. And pie. Banoffee to be exact—a favorite from when I lived in England. I slept a bit fitfully that night, I think my body was aching for the mineral pools. But I've found that the last night is always the hardest—my mind a battleground combating the desire to stay with the sweet pull of home. The next morning, I played in the photo booth in the lobby of the hotel and finished desert dining with a perfect breakfast sandwich, and a slice of to-go pie to keep me company while I packed for home.

BRING IT HOME: SUCCULENT GARDEN

From Joshua Tree I brought home the desire and willingness to be better to my indoor plants. It seems a strange impulse, espe-

cially coming from the desert landscape, but it was the life in the desert that inspired me. Yucca has a particular talent for spreading quickly after wildfires—a testament to the perpetual cycle and renewal of life. It was really that ideology that I carried home. In my work toward self-care and preser-

vation, I have found confronting the darkness to be important work. Succulents, cacti, and yucca remind me how little we truly need in order to carry on—just abundant light and a little nourishment. My heart is healed by these reminders, and my home is a temple to these reflections.

8

TRAVELING WITH YOUR BEST FRIEND// IRELAND

ONCE UPON A TIME, I flew across the great cerulean ocean and set my feet, and my spirit, upon the verdant island of Ireland. Those of us—and we are indeed an army unto ourselves—that claim Irish blood, find traveling to the country an almost religious experience. Prominent Catholic culture aside, something deeper resonates in the depths of our being, something that connects spiritually and emotionally to the lush life that blankets that island in the Irish Sea. Natives look at you with a mixed expression of sympathy and amusement when you share your lineage because in truth, while I can feel the Irish blood run with heated pulse through my body, I'm an American. And they know it. But that does not deter from the experience of traveling to what my best friend Amy and I affectionately call the motherland.

Ten years ago, Amy and I were sitting in a little café in the city where we were both raised. After great adventures coast to

coast and the world over, we both found ourselves living once again in Omaha, Nebraska. Over greasy eggs and burnt toast I looked across the table at her and said simply, "I want to go to Ireland . . . and I want to go with you." We've been best friends since we were thirteen and even have a tattoo to prove it. The idea of running away together—even for a week and especially over the expanse of the churning waters of the Atlantic—lit a fire in our hearts. But we didn't go to Ireland. We traveled to Italy together twice after that breakfast, once to accompany her at a printmaking residency, the following summer just because. We made a trek to Marrakech the next year and decided then we would try to get away together once a year until we couldn't walk anymore, ideally when we are 105 years old. When the question of where to next was presented, Ireland seemed the answer, naturally.

MY JOURNAL

We arrived with a cocktail of excitement and exhaustion clouding our vision, but were eager to explore our first stop, the fine city of Dublin. Rambling through the streets to find ourselves in the Victorian splendor of St. Stephen's Green, we took up a patch of grass with the locals and sat in the warm sun for over an hour. Amy and I have spent the majority of our adult lives living many miles from one another. Though we spent the first few hours of our flight tumbling over our words with excitement and relish, so happy to be together again, it was the open space and beauty of that park that allowed us to breathe into the idea that we were here for each other. Cherished friends, the ones who really get you; the friends whose emotional and spiritual depth mirror your own; the relationships you cannot fathom living without—those must be

cultivated, cared for, and never taken for granted. That was what this trip to-gether was all about really. Spending time together on this adventure was our way of saying, "thank you" and "you are so special to me." That moment in the park set the tone for the rest of our week.

We made the most of our short time in the city. We wandered through the quiet corridors of the Trinity College Library to luxuriate in the illuminated glow of the Book of Kells. We visited the heartbreakingly underfunded Natural History Museum—a walk through a cabinet of curiosities. We had a perfect lunch of fish-and-chips, and we lingered over cappuccinos as we waited for the rush of afternoon rain to pass. But the road was calling.

Ireland is green. But in June, it is positively emerald. The skies were linen gray and softened the bright hedgerows as we wound our way over the dales toward Kilkenny. After a day of sightseeing, I was ready to take to the luxury linens in our riverside hotel, but Amy insisted we search out a modern-day minstrel. Just across the street from our lodging we found a small pub and two seats at the bar, right in front of the crooning performer. Many an Irish whiskey later into the evening and we were singing out loud, laughing so hard we nearly lost our seating, and needed a moonlit detour to clear our heads enough for slumber. Amy and I have had a number of these moments—that crack in time when skirting excess leads to unleashing the weight of our daily anxieties. Being an adult is hard and giving ourselves the space and allowance to simply let go once in a while is important, whether that involves libations or not is a personal choice. But traveling with your best friend is the best excuse.

The June sun breaks early in Ireland, and it coaxed us back on the meander-ing route leading to the village of Oughterard off the western shore. A small cottage nestled near the banks of the Owenriff River awaited our arrival. We shared the land with our host, who resided in the main house, and two Conne-mara ponies, whose presence set the notion that magic resided in this place. The lazy afternoons at the cottage found us preparing our own meals of fresh greens and smoked salmon with homemade maple dressing, taking lingering walks and becoming deliciously lost in the manicured shrubberies and gravel paths of the village, resting near rushing brooks, and chasing a sun that filtered through the greens like a dream as the dark hedges hummed their ageless secrets. We kept the ponies company while we sketched and wrote each evening. Short day trips from the cottage found us in Clifden, for Celtic-inspired silver and a dinner of mussels and chips, and Roundstone, a beach so spectacular in hue, you can hardly believe your eyes.

Wanting, needing really, to see as much of the country as possible, we took those picturesque roads once more to the seaside town of Portrush in Northern Ireland. A jewel of a bed-and-breakfast awaited, and the stay allowed us easy access to the crisp summer shore and a fine drive about the precipice of the northern coast. Rain kissed our summer skin at every stop, and instead of dampening our experience, we felt the moist air was welcoming us with whispered charms. Almost always, the rain would give way to the softest sun, embraced by the silkiest of clouds.

Back on the road, we made our way to the Hill of Tara and Newgrange, two of the most enchanting places in the country. The Hill of Tara dates back to the crowning of the High Kings before Patrick converted the Isle, and Newgrange predates history itself. Our anchor in the area was the historic Bellinter House in Navan, and after such moving afternoons exploring, a soak in the copper tub and whiskey in the drawing room were a welcome balm for the soul.

Tara is a small village in county Meath, and in the boundaries of its land-scape sits the Hill of Tara. "Mounds" are not uncommon in Ireland, but Tara's significance lies in her royal history. It was once believed to be the dwelling place of the great goddess Maeve who alone could bestow the crown upon the High King. The earth vibrates with ancient power on this rolling panorama, and the views of the countryside below must have been especially potent on celebrations such as Beltane, where bonfires would have glowed against a blanket of stars as the Celts celebrated the coming of summer. Upon one mound grows a Wishing Tree. The power of Tara is infectious, and the Wishing Tree stands as a testament to that. Visitors tie their wishes to her seemingly enchanted branches with whatever they carry—gum wrappers, socks, baby pacifiers, bits of ribbon, truly anything you can imagine can be found entan-gled in her limbs. However, the idea is not to leave something behind, but to beseech the ancient land for guidance or gifts of the heart. We left our wishes there, and I can tell you without reservation: mine came true.

Just over the dale stands Newgrange, a holy mound also located in beauti-ful county Meath and believed to be older than Stonehenge and the Egyptian pyramids. Originally used for ceremonies and burials, Newgrange is also home to the original triple spiral, which has in turn become a nationally recognized symbol in Ireland. While scholars politely disagree about the true meaning of the triple spiral, the most common interpretation is the three realms (land, sea, and sky). Others believe its meaning is deeper—the Triple Goddess, the

stages of fertility, and the symbol of seasons themselves. I particularly love our guide's thoughts on the matter: who I was, who I am, and who I am meant to be. I find it important to seek out history when traveling. Seeking out ancient relics, museums, sacred tombs, and places of worship connect me on a visceral level with the surroundings and deepens my experience profoundly.

To say that we were moved by the power of Ireland is a gross understatement. Amy and I held hands and shared tears as our plane lifted off the tarmac, homeward bound, from Dublin. We called and texted each other daily for weeks, almost as if we'd left something behind in the mist of the isle, something we desperately needed to retrieve. How could I hold on to those moments, those memories, but also the spellbound rapture I had found in the ancient lands of my ancestors?

BRING IT HOME: THE WISHING TREE

My husband, children, and I moved into our new home as a blended family a few years ago. As the eight of us settled into a life together, it was important to me to create spaces that felt special to each member of our family. We love being together—whether at nightly family dinners around the table my husband hand-built or game nights in our living room—but with a large family, personal space is of equal importance.

The children each have their favorite corners of our home, but I wanted to create an outdoor refuge as well. The Wishing Tree was incredibly inspirational to me in this regard. We choose a medium-size tree on the backside of our property and each tied a wish to its branches in a symbolic rite of welcoming the tree to a higher calling. Since that day, the children will often take haven under her limbs to read, draw, and write—and wish.

BRING IT HOME: GUINNESS BROWN BREAD

I travel not only to expose my body and soul to other cultures and the magic that permeates the air the world over, but in hopes of bringing some part of my experience and new knowledge home to stay. Brown bread is a staple in Irish kitchens, and for good reason. Because the bread does not require yeast, it's relatively quick to make. And its hearty personality makes for a solid breakfast, whether making one's way to the fields or the office to work for the day. We were welcomed in nearly every place we stayed with a loaf of brown bread and the only way to eat it, as far as I'm concerned, is with a healthy slather of Irish butter. My personal favorite recipe was at Shola Coach House in county Antrim. Don't be afraid to ask for a recipe when traveling, especially if you've fallen in love with what you are experiencing. If the kitchen is not ready to trade its secrets, take notes about what you're tasting—the texture, the serving portion—as it will help you recreate the flavors upon your return home. Thankfully, owners Sharon and David Schindler were happy to share their recipe for Guinness Brown Bread, and it's become one of my favorite souvenirs.

GUINNESS BROWN BREAD

4 tablespoons butter

1 tablespoon maple syrup

2 ounces water

12 ounces Extra Stout Guinness

⅛ cup steel-cut oats

3 cups plus 2 tablespoons whole wheat flour

4 tablespoons demerara sugar

2 tablespoons baking soda

1. Preheat the oven to 375°F. Lightly grease a loaf pan and set it aside.

2. Heat the butter and syrup in a saucepan over low heat until melted. Add the water and Guinness and whisk thoroughly.

3. Combine the oats, flour, and sugar in a mixing bowl. Sift in the baking soda and mix well.

4. Add the wet ingredients to the dry and mix well. Transfer to the prepared loaf pan and bake for 45 minutes. The middle of the bread will rise slightly and once removed from the pan, the loaf will sound hollow if tapped on the bottom.

5. Wrap in a clean towel and allow the loaf to cool. Slice and enjoy with copious amounts of Irish butter.

9

TRAVELING WITH A GROUP OF FRIENDS // ICELAND

ICELAND IS ANOTHER PLANET. A moonscape of ice blue, jet black, and neon green. A common statement made about the country is that it's otherworldly. And it is in so many ways. Paganism still has a strong hold on the island. According to a BBC News article from 2015, neo-paganism is the fastest-growing religion on the island. Followers of the Asatru faith worship as their ancestors once did, praising the pantheon of the Norse gods.

It was this magic, surreal beauty, and ethereal charm that led me to accept a position to colead a visual storytelling workshop through The Hill Workshops. Nadia Dole hosts artistic retreats around the world, and she is an infectious spirit. Several of my closest girlfriends wanted to make this trip as desperately as I, and we found ourselves on this planet of opposing wonders. When planning a trip with a group, it's important to truly know who you're traveling with. When thinking about my closest girlfriends, we share tastes in food, drink, aesthetics, and design,

and that makes for an easy trip. But more importantly, we share a deep love and respect for one another. We care about each other's well-being. And that is of the utmost importance. Finding a group of friends who balance each other, look out for one another, and lack ego when making group decisions is truly a gift.

In the opening chapter, I spoke about how important having a plan is to a successful road trip. But there are times, when you are with people you trust, that you may feel a little more comfortable taking chances, seeing where a road may lead. Iceland stands as a reminder that regardless of foresight and planning, unexpected adventures can always be found. The difference between an adventure and unforeseen circumstances is simply your perception. Be open, be flexible, and remember to always be safe.

MY JOURNAL

Our first stop was the famous Blue Lagoon just outside of the country's capital of Reykjavík and we were starving—a quick lunch of smoked salmon sandwiches with hard-boiled eggs, tomatoes, and honey mustard on a sesame-studded baguette fueled us before making our way to the steaming lagoon. We floated for hours, photographed each other in the opaque blue lagoon, and watched as mud-faced tourists moved eerily through the baby-blue water and steam clouds. It was a beautiful afternoon and we took our time, our bodies weary from the international flight. We sat in a cave and met a family from Florida; we drank Prosecco from a swim-up bar; we swam in the rain and stood beneath a waterfall. It was the ideal welcome to this strange land.

With our limbs lax and our bodies warm and glowing, we retreated to the hotel for a respite in our adjacent rooms—some of us needing quiet space away from the crowds of the pools, others simply cherishing the opportunity to keep such lovely company.

As we began to pack the car in the morning, a double rainbow appeared over the lagoon—an omen for the amazing day that lay before us. Taking breakfast in the hotel before our drive, I realized how inspired I was by not only how Europeans take their morning meals, but Icelanders in particular. Breakfast was smoked salmon, an array of hard and soft cheeses, boiled eggs, brown bread and honey, and anise- and cinnamon-spiked fish. At that moment, I knew what I would be bringing back from Iceland: breakfast inspiration.

Our drive to Seljalandsfoss—a collection of waterfalls, one magnanimous, and the others accompanying its symphony—was punctuated by gray skies.

Slashes of sunlight would often stab their way across the open landscape only to be followed by a downpour of rain. Ancient man-made caves dotted the road; vivid green fields were studded with horses and sheep. We went on a breathtaking hike to the top of Skogafoss, a truly majestic waterfall, with mist on our faces, wild wind fingering our hair, and birds nearly within reach.

Every area of Iceland seemed to be infused with more power than the last. It was our first full day on the island, and we could not get enough. After checking into our hotel in Vik, we made our way back out to the Black Beach. Black steps rose from the sands, and granite-washed caves hid about the surf. The sea itself foamed in crystal bubbles over jet-black rocks—frozen black beasts that seemed to rise from the ocean depths. Our hearts and heads made dizzying efforts to absorb what we had experienced that day.

For many years, I have taken landscapes for granted. I was drawn to the cities, culture, museums, restaurants that topped editor's lists, and stores that were the cult-obsessed darlings of glossy magazines. As I get older, I want to celebrate the land—the wild places that conjure emotion deep within my soul. I have found over the years that if I'm seeking a deeper sense of self and desire to experience a world truly outside of my own, I seek the wilds.

As morning stretched her fingers across the island, we found ourselves so eager to arrive at the farmhouse in Reykholt, which would be our base for the next few days, that we drove straight through without stopping. The following day, we followed our group caravan-style into the heart of the West Fjords, all for a bowl of soup. In an effort to go against the guidebook and have us experience Iceland as if we lived there, Nadia, our workshop coordinator, led us on a long, awe-inspiring hike along the black craggy coast to a small village for golden seafood soup and olive-studded rolls. That cold, wet, and windy hike was worth every moment. Our group was made up of men and women between

twenty and nearly seventy years of age. And again, I had to reflect on the importance of traveling with people who are patient, respectful, and simply good. We helped each other over questionable footing and embraced one another as we entered the village. The hike took us past both an old elf village and a dragon lair—how could the soup not be magic?

Our adventure then took an unexpected detour: a harrowing drive up the side of a mountain to visit a famous glacier. We drove through the clouds—dark, heavy, wet clouds—with mountain sheep, streams of milky water, and black rocks suddenly emerging from the haunting landscape. Then the glacier glowed through the mists—and we disappeared. As the sinking sun teased us beyond the mist, we began our long, dark drive back to the farm along crashing ice waves and mountain roads. Often the road leads to unexpected adventures, but that evening, as we all retold our personal experience during our midnight dinner of shakshuka and red wine, it was mixed with awe, gratitude, and laughter. It was the first time traveling that I came together with a group of friends that could articulate what the day had brought them so well, both physically and emotionally. It was a beautiful shared familiarity and one that has since encouraged me to look for further experiences traveling with a group of like-minded individuals.

On our final day in the West Fjords, we took to the back roads of the country and headed straight for the iconic Golden Circle, which we immediately bypassed. Our friend and fearless leader Nadia wanted our experience to be as much off the beaten path as we could imagine. We had planned a simple picnic and, as the temperatures dropped unexpectedly and the wind began to softly howl, that plan was looking like it might be in jeopardy. We traveled in a caravan of three vehicles, and none of us really knew where we were going. We pulled off several times, awaited the lead car to turn off the engine and un-pile, but no, we pulled back onto the road again and again. Finally, we followed a turn signal to the right and pulled into a small field. Just beyond the clearing was a circle of trees protecting picnic tables from the wind, and past that, a waterfall. A beautiful stream kept us company as we feasted on smoked salmon salad, cured meats, hard and butter-soft cheeses, olives, and figs. We drank cider and wrapped ourselves in blankets and laughed at our luck. Bellies full and wonder still glowing in the air, a rustle was heard across the stream. And there came six wild Icelandic horses—magnificent creatures that seemed to have emerged from the mist. We walked among them, guests in their magical realm, knowing that we were sharing a moment that would live among us forever.

BRING IT HOME: ICELANDIC BREAKFAST

Having traveled all over Europe and the Mediterranean in my twenties, I remember being struck at how differently breakfast was served in comparison to my own relationship with the first meal of the day. With the copious spreads of meats, cheeses, jams, yogurts, fruits, and breads laid out in the hotels each morning, my first instinct was not so much to savor the uniqueness of the experience, but to eat as much as possible to avoid spending my limited budget on lunch while I ran from museum to museum. That naïve perspective shifted only after I returned to Europe many years later. I leaned to cherish the thought and art of such feasts. I finally understood the practicality of a breakfast full of proteins and energy-laden choices. And to be perfectly honest, it can be a strikingly beautiful way to lay out a meal. Icelandic breakfasts reminded me of my deep love for this way of eating. Through a desire to expose my children to a variety of cultural customs and my restless need to create memorable traditions for our family, we now enjoy an Icelandic breakfast once a month. The kids even eat the smoked fish.

10

TRAVELING WITH YOUR PARTNER // BLUE RIDGE MOUNTAINS + PAWLEYS ISLAND

GETTING AWAY IS HARD when you have children. It doesn't matter if you have one child . . . or in our case, six. It takes a great deal of coordinating, planning, and wishful thinking to make even the quickest getaways come together. My husband and I are incredibly grateful for the time we have—though rare and often short—to take a trip together. We both believe that taking time to honor each other is a vital component of an efficacious marriage. Whether your relationship with your partner is a newly budding stem or spans decades, whether it's just the two of you or a household of little ones, time away together is so important. Our lives are chaotic and we must choose to prioritize those people that we have elected to share our lives with. Date nights are lovely, but escaping the norm, even for a night for two, can be transformative and an important reminder of our sacred connection with each other.

JUST A NIGHT IN THE
BLUE RIDGE MOUNTAINS

KOLI AND I CELEBRATED our anniversary with a night at the same inn where we had shared our thirty-six-hour honeymoon (see afore-mentioned children). Although our time away was brief, we took advantage of our drive up into the mountains skirting the Tennessee border.

MY JOURNAL

The Blue Ridge Mountains are named such because it looks like they've cut midnight- and smoky-blue ridges across the sky. Great, gray mists cling to their form, and in the fall, when the trees are bursting with the colors of fire, it's an incredible sight. We made our way leisurely through the twists and turns of the back roads, small towns beckoning us to stay for a moment to explore their curiosities. Rock shops and antiques, farmer's markets and artisan grocers—I love exploring the offerings of small-town America. We arrived at the Mast Farm Inn in Valle Crucis in the late afternoon and set to settling into the generous sofa in front of the woodstove fireplace.

Days before our trip, I had returned from traveling the road along Kentucky's Bourbon Trail with my mother, aunt, and cousin. Still floating on memories of handsome distilleries, the delicious burn of whiskey, and the scent that punctuates the air there (like the most heavenly of bakeries), we brought several bottles of bourbon to enjoy. We opened each and poured them out like flights, tasting, comparing, and discussing as they warmed our bellies. We laughed, we loved, and we honored us.

BRING IT HOME: GEMS AND MINERALS

Before we followed the road home, we found ourselves atop the world on Grandfather Mountain, the highest peak in the Blue Ridge Mountains. The air was brilliant and the view clear and bright. Wandering through the nature preserve and museum, we were both drawn to a large specimen of rutilated quartz in one of the cases. Clear with golden streaks of rutilite, this member of the quartz family is believed to manifest desires, stabilize love, and attract beauty and happiness to one's life. Finding our own specimen felt like a beautiful and symbolic way to remember our trip to the mountains, so we decided a quick stop on our way home at the rock shop in Spruce Pine, North Carolina, was necessary.

A BIT
LONGER ON
PAWLEYS ISLAND

OUR FIRST TRUE VACATION together was to the beach. Pawleys Island is part of the Atlantic coast barrier islands in South Carolina. Just an hour from Charleston's cobbled-street beauty and a solid forty-five minutes from the craziness of Myrtle Beach's boardwalks, there is nowhere I'd rather summer on the East Coast than this quiet beachside village. Our time at the inn was self-imposed relaxation. Like so many parents, our days seem endless and then sort of all mashed together at the end of the week in a frenzied blur. When we do find pockets of time to ourselves, we often find that laundry needs folding, floors need sweeping, rugs need vacuuming, or recycling needs sorting. But we have worked hard at remembering how important "we" are. Not just getting away together, but taking moments during the week for each other. It's not only for the sake of our marriage, but for the way we want our children to view love. Every gesture, every word is full of power; we take care to ensure that we are showing our children through our actions that love is about gratitude, patience, understanding, and empathy. Unconditional love is our legacy. And with that in mind we drove to South Carolina.

MY JOURNAL

The drive from the mountains is magic—descending from the Blue Ridges into the flat plateau of the Piedmont and the sticky, sweet warmth of the South Carolina marshes. We pulled into the small gravel drive at the Pelican Inn just in time for a homemade supper. Built in 1840, the inn has changed ownership only a handful of times in its long history as both a private guesthouse and public inn. Today it's lovingly cared for by Corinne Taylor and her family from Atlanta, Georgia, who stay the summer to turn down all the beds, cook every meal, and share ghost stories if you ask.

It's hard for us to get away, and there is often an unspoken pressure to do something, anything really, to ensure our time away is well spent. But, I have found that as I ever so gracefully age into my forties, that pressure has morphed into another idea . . . one of doing absolutely nothing. There are city vacations in which the desire to experience the lights, the dishes, the people, will coax me out of bed every morning ready to explore. But there are other road trips, those that lead to quiet places that encourage my heart and body's demand at restoration. Our trip to the beach was such an escape. We slept until the sun was quite comfortable in the morning sky—only to rise at the call of the breakfast bell each morning. After satisfying our hunger with homemade biscuits, hot bacon, and piles of scrambled eggs, we would often not make it back to the solitude of our room, but collapse together in an oversized hammock where slumber might sneak upon us once more.

Our second night on the island, we bellied up to a cherrywood bar for baskets of fried seafood, ice-cold beer, and live music. The heat of the day was just

beginning to ebb and, as the strung lights on the outside patio began to glow, the dirt lot seemed to suddenly swell with cars. This was the place to be. Teeming with locals and tourists in the know, we were happy strangers among a sea of familiar faces. That night we walked down to the beach where the stars blazed across the sky like a dark blanket of diamond dust. We discovered ghost crabs—small, white crustaceans that pop up in the dark and move like lightening striking across the sand. I retreated to a hammock on the dune and watched my husband's flashlight seek out these little apparitions on the beach below.

Our days were spent with salt clinging to our locks and sand on our feet. Just as it does every morning, the bell rings once more in the afternoon to signal lunch. We were served family style, as if you are a personal guest of the owner; bare feet and damp swimsuits were not only accepted, but seemingly embraced. My favorite meal that week was sharing a table with an older couple who'd been coming to the inn for nearly twenty years, and two sisters, one a celebrated painter, who were experiencing the Pelican for the first time. We ate a Louisiana shrimp boil with our hands, soaked our hot, buttery rolls in the juice left behind, and capped the meal with an incredibly special chocolate pie.

Our last day, and a summer storm rolled angrily across the sky. We found ourselves on the marsh-side of the property in a tin-roofed crabbing shack. Koli was crabbing and I was reading in a hammock when the rain began. We were stuck out there for over an hour and the sound of the rain hammering the roof was deafening. And then it was as if the sky was a heavy gray canvas split with a knife—the sun poured through and we were treated to a spectacularly colorful sunset, and we realized that this was one of the few road trips that was truly about the destination.

BRING IT HOME: AN OUTDOOR SANCTUARY

Koli and I spent hours in the hammocks at the Pelican Inn. We napped in them alone but more often in each other's embrace. We read, and spoke of our days together, our children, their future, and the gift and challenge of raising a large family. We laughed in those hammocks; we drank bourbon and watched the stars. Upon returning home, Koli built a fire pit and bench seating in our backyard. While he labored moving heavy rocks and constructing our seating to surround the fire, I cleared years of overgrowth and weeds from our gardens. And I discovered two trees, roughly of the same build and character, separated by about twelve feet. The perfect place for a hammock.

11

TRAVELING WITH YOUR FAMILY// YELLOWSTONE + OUTER BANKS

N 1983, MY PARENTS, brother, and I piled into our big, fancy conversion van and drove from Omaha, Nebraska, to Cincinnati, Ohio, to spend Thanksgiving with my grandparents. That trip proved to be among the greatest travel memories of my youth. Upon our return, a crippling snow and ice storm stretched its angry arms across the Plains and after hours of creeping at five miles an hour through Iowa, my parents decided the situation was simply too dangerous to continue. We checked into a Holiday Inn (Holidome as they were known in the eighties thanks to the large glass, domed atriums where the pool and minigolf were located) at the next exit. And there, in Davenport, Iowa, we camped out for the next three days. No swimsuits had been packed, but they sold disposable plastic suits in a vending machine and those would have to do. We spent most of the day swimming and subsequently dumping excess water out of our suits whenever we made way for the slide or waterfall. We took

every meal in the hotel's modest restaurant and dined on cheeseburgers without the burger because the delivery truck was stuck on the interstate. I clearly remember thinking that this was the best time I'd ever had. A large part of that was because my parents treated those three days as an unexpected adventure and made us feel lucky to experience that time together. I share this story because as parents we often have unrealistic expectations about traveling with our children. And the truth is . . . children are incredibly adaptable and flexible. They look to us as a barometer for their thresholds. Be prepared with a solid plan, but always be ready for an unexpected adventure.

YELLOWSTONE

I HAVE TALKED ABOUT HOW travel changes you. Sometimes, it changes everything around you as well. Often we cannot see the storms we've brewed until we have removed ourselves from our homes and familiar communities; only when we leave do the realization and acknowledgment settle upon our shoulders. We also may not realize the deep significance of a journey until much later. Such was my trip across the United States with my family in

2014. It was the last road trip my ex-husband and I would take together with our daughters. I'm grateful for not only the time we spent together on the road, but also the opportunity to look at ourselves and our life together with honesty and, eventually, gratitude and understanding. Oddly enough, this was one of the few trips in my life that I did not keep a written journal. But I kept a thorough visual record and looking at those photographs brings to life the memories both striking and sore. I can look at a photograph of a chair on a porch, warmed with a blanket and coffee beckoning, and recall exactly what I was thinking—knowing even then the answers my heart was too terrified to accept. This is why keeping a travel record is so important. Whether by word, sketch, or photograph, time around you dissolves and you are back on that porch. But you now have the gift of perspective and insight; you were *there*, now you are *here*. Look at all that you've learned and how you've grown. This is ultimately one of the greatest gifts of travel.

MY JOURNAL

I love the road west. I took it for granted when I was younger, when we took so many trips between Omaha and California, then Omaha and Colorado, then Omaha and Arizona. It was a drive I felt I could execute in my sleep. Then I moved east and, after several years, felt a deep ache for those open, tree-bare stretches of highway. I wanted the girls to experience the West as I remembered it—vast, unforgiving landscapes, the wilds of our great nation still open and seemingly limitless.

In Montana, our first stay was at a guest ranch just outside of Bozeman. The evening we arrived we were welcomed by the horses on the property and the scent of roast pork in the air for the once-a-week barbeque the ranch hosts for all its guests. Dining creek side with mountain vistas, beer and barbeque, and live music was the perfect welcome after a long day on the road. Our cabin overlooked a wide mountain stream and our morning views were often framed in mists with the occasional bald eagle breaking through the haze. We drank coffee on the front porch as the sun broke and then dressed for the fresh eggs, sausage, and potatoes that beckoned at the main lodge.

We spent one day exploring the town of Bozeman and watching my daughter Aela capture everything she could with her camera. But the most memorable of our days were spent in Yellowstone with its shifting landscapes, Technicolor geothermal springs, roadside American buffalo, roaring waterfalls, and quiet valleys. I don't recall the girls asking even once, "Are we there yet?" They realized that the moment we crossed into the national park, we'd arrived. We spent a lot of time those days in the car, driving through scenic vistas and

taking shelter from a rainstorm or two. But through our hikes and exploration of the area—even waiting an hour for the infamous Old Faithful to explode into the blinding blue sky—the girls showed an enormous amount of patience. We returned to the cabin early on our last evening at the ranch to prepare a sunset dinner by the creek. And while our roast chicken and potatoes warmed our bellies, it was dessert that we were all waiting for: mountain pies in the moonlight aside a dancing fire.

We spent our last night in Montana at Yellowstone Under Canvas, glamping. While I sort of loathe that word, I only started camping in the last ten years, and I'm that woman who drags along the air mattress and real linens for the back room of our tent, and the little portable potty for the front room. So I get the glamping concept. Under Canvas takes it to another level—one of several companies catering to those of us who'd rather have a bit more comfort in the great outdoors, their canvas tents are built on platforms, feature wood flooring, king-size beds, and occasionally, full bathrooms and woodstoves. The price of a single night could easily place you in five-star accommodations in Manhattan, but the experience is well worth the price tag. The Yellowstone location resembles a tent city—and electric fences surround the property to keep the bears and wolves at bay—but it's in the middle of the wilds and it feels safe, comforting, and is something I dream of doing again. The girls ran about the property, relaxed into their books, worked on their journals—it was the most settled I had seen them on the entire trip.

We worked our way back east with a quick drive through the stunningly beautiful Grand Tetons and a short hike along the shore of Jenny Lake, after which we rushed back to the car to change into swimsuits. We spent a long afternoon splashing in the cool water, picnicking, and talking about what we had experienced that week.

Our drive to Yellowstone was full of self-reflection and questions I was not quite ready to answer. But the utter joy and curiosity that my daughters revealed over the few weeks of travel—the way they stood in awe of the power of nature and every little reaction brought forth from their wondering eyes, delighted smiles, and excited lips—reminded me why we had planned this trip in the first place. Regardless of anxieties and stress, this trip was truly a time to live in the moment. That is what a family vacation is all about.

BRING IT HOME: COWBOY BOOTS

My first pair of real cowboy boots was a high school graduation gift in 1993. I grew up in Omaha, Nebraska, and the cityscape was just beginning to shift—both literally and figuratively in the early nineties. When my parents moved there from Maryland in 1980, it was still a stock-yard town. My parents adopted

the music, the boots, and the shearling jackets with enthusiasm. Copious amounts of money have since flooded Omaha, making it only a glimpse of what it once was. But I still own my Great Plains roots and always feel comfortable in cowboy boots. And is there anywhere more authentic to buy cowboy boots than in the American West? Okay, maybe Texas. Along with our new boots, we brought home an appreciation for the heritage of the Wild West. Every time we slip them on, we're reminded of the open spaces of Wyoming and Montana—and it solidifies our desire to return.

OUTER BANKS

MY PARENTS FELL IN LOVE on the Outer Banks of North Carolina. It is an incredibly special place, especially to my mother, as we lived there when I was toddler—directly under the shadow of the Cape Hatteras Lighthouse. We started spending our winters on the beaches of Rodanthe, after all of my siblings moved south, to celebrate my father's birthday, which falls just two days after the New Year. Near the one-year anniversary of his death, we wanted to honor what would have been his seventy-fifth birthday with one last trip.

In 2014, still reeling from an impending divorce, I truly, for the first time in my life, allowed myself to fall apart when my dad died. He was the greatest man I knew. His shared love story with my mother is what everyone wishes upon the stars to experience; his quiet strength, unconditional love, and the core of his character helped shape the woman I'm still in the process of becoming. The loss was so great that the gaping wound in my chest will likely never heal. It becomes a little easier to live with as the days pass, but a photograph, a scent, a song can send a gust of cold air through that space and it feels as if we lost him yesterday.

My focus became my mother and my family. My ex-husband and I made the life-altering decision to continue working on our relationship outside of our marriage and we now have more

love, patience, gratitude, and understanding for each other than we ever did when we were married. Healing was complex as it was intertwined with multiple layers of grieving and watching my mother try to function without the other half of her soul. This was never more evident than the week we spent without him on the Outer Banks.

It was also our first family vacation for my husband and our blended family of six children. A mutual friend had introduced Koli and me the year before, and within weeks of our first date, our children were meeting, within months we were looking at houses together, and before the end of the year we were married. We kept taking careful steps back, questioning the authenticity of what was happening to us and wanting to ensure that

our strong feelings for each other and our children were not filling voids or an attempt to replace losses. But they were not. We found in each other something that we never thought possible: the ability to communicate so openly and safely—the complete absence of ego—and unconditional love for each other and our children. So we blended.

It was that experience, that deep love that blossomed from the depths of my being, that allowed me to navigate that week in Rodanthe.

MY JOURNAL

Upon arrival, we immediately set foot to sand as we raced for the shoreline. I love winter beaches—the water is cold, the sand a bit harder, and the wind often unforgiving. But the beaches are nearly empty, yours alone to explore. We collected seashells, played tag, chased each other through the wind, and slid down dunes—stretching our legs after the trek across the state. The light was beautiful, a glowing wash of pinks and baby blues bleeding through a soft haze. It was the welcome we craved, and that night we made a feast of local shrimp and raw oysters—the children's fascination and disgust seriously amusing to my husband, mother, and I who relished every slurp.

The following days were spent in and out of the house, a delicate dance of creating and crushing the space between all of us. Thursday morning, I woke early and drove north from Rodanthe along the Outer Banks to the Bodie Lighthouse. The morning was thick with fog, and I sat in the car watching the light of the structure cross the sky in its repetitive pattern. It occurred to me, in a rather poetic way, that the light always pushes through. That lighthouse stood as an illuminated reminder that the pain we were still processing would not always cloud our vision. For the first time on that trip I allowed myself to cry; it was therapeutic and reawakened the light in my own chest . . . that beacon led me back to the house where my family still slept.

Saturday, the sun finally poked through the heavy sky, and we ventured down the strand to a pirate museum. The kids uncoiled themselves from the tangles of scarves and winter coats to set about exploring the building and completing a scavenger hunt set up by the museum. We stuffed ourselves with

fried seafood that afternoon before making our way to the lighthouse where the kids stamped their National Park Passports and chased each other around the base of the black and white giant. When we returned to the house, the children sat in front of the fire and warmed their toes while debating who the most fearsome pirate among them might be. Later that night I stole a moment alone with Koli as we sunk our bodies into the hot tub under the stars, the waves crashing nearby.

Our road trip to the beach was punctuated with equal parts joy and heartache, and it was a lesson in absolute love, grief, patience, and acceptance. We worked hard at making every moment of that trip count for our children. And this trip was captured in photographs more than words—the words were difficult then, and they are difficult today. But when I look at the images I captured that week, I see the joy in my children, the warmth and love in my husband, and the hope and healing in my mother, and I know that it was a road trip I will forever be thankful for. The road always leads to personal evolution, whether that be apparent immediately or in time; your heart, soul, and mind will shape-shift.

BRING IT HOME: COFFEE MUGS

My father couldn't function without coffee. In reality, I'm sure he could—but he didn't want to. He drank it all day long, and I will never forget my first time home after living in Italy when I brewed him his first stovetop espresso. His eyes glowed with delight and before I served his second cup, he was online ordering his own percolator. He never did use the thing, preferring the quick accessibility of the single-serve machines. Our home on the Outer Banks featured an unobstructed view of the Rodanthe Pier, and most mornings, my father and I were the first awake and we would sit on the back porch in rocking chairs, watching the waves crash against the weakened wooden legs of the pier as the sky turned from rose and ginger to cerulean blue. We drank copious amounts of coffee and he would talk to me about his Navy days, about the great questions of life . . . about anything that came to his brilliant mind. And he would always talk about me—about how proud he was, about the gratitude he felt for both my mother and his granddaughters. We drank from simple porcelain mugs that my mother had purchased in a gift shop down the road featuring the emblem of the U.S. Life-Saving Service. Those mugs bring me great joy, and I still sip my coffee from them daily, his memory a warm cloak about my shoulders every morning.

12

DAY TRIP //
A FOREST PICNIC

MY FAVORITE DAY TRIPS are spontaneous, "let's pile in the car and see where the road takes us" sort of days. "Let us open our arms to adventure and be ready for anything" sort of days. I am lucky enough to live somewhere that beckons exploration. Growing up on the Great Plains, I believed there was not much to sightsee in my home-town. I know now, through years of perspective, that's not nec-essarily true.

My first experience with being comfortable jumping into a car and just exploring was living on the small island of La Madd-alena, Italy, in my early twenties. I was serving with the US Navy on a ship stationed there and, to be truthful, at that point joining the Navy was the most adventurous step I'd ever taken on my own. And La Maddalena complemented that newfound spirit in me fiercely. Hidden beaches, tiny portside towns, and country-side *agriturismos* were just some of my finds, and they sparked something I had never quite experienced. I discovered a sense of wonder and a belief that there is so much in my own community and the wilds of my own backyard to explore. It is a reason I love living in the mountains of western North Carolina. It also gives me so much joy to raise our children with this passion for exploration. We head into the mountains or forests as much as we can. Hidden swimming holes are my heart's delight, and there is always a picnic ready to go in the back of the car. I've written a lot about planning your road trips and about being prepared. But day trips are the perfect excuse to throw the maps out the window (figuratively, of course).

MY JOURNAL

A balmy summer Saturday is always our ideal excuse to take to the woods.
Though the road to Pisgah National Forest is not too far from our home on the
south side of Asheville, the kids are always anxious to arrive. Aside from our
destination and the picnic in the back seat, we have no solid plans, and the kids
giggle with anticipation. To keep the spontaneity easy, I try to keep a go-to list
of what we pack on our day trips. It makes packing up the car quick and limits
the likelihood of forgetting something. Today, I brought real plates and Mason
jar cups; I serve tea in glass jugs and bring along antique flatware; I tote linens
and sometimes candles. I have the kids gather leaves and twigs to decorate our
table. None of this is required or necessary, but it makes a beautiful tablescape
and the children love to help set up our feasts. We eat, we explore, we swim—
and we eat again. After a chill begins to touch the air, we pack away our picnic
and start off on a trailhead we know well that leads to a cave and waterfall.
Watching the children chase each other through the woods, wet hair splayed
across their backs, feet and legs muddy, I feel grateful that in these moments
I have swallowed the need to dictate every moment. These are the summer
days I crave the most . . . when we all have the rare ability to let go completely.
A stop for ice cream on the way home at Dolly's, the iconic Brevard institution,
was a must, just because it always feels like the perfect way to cap a day.

BRING IT HOME: PICNIC FAVORITES

Here I share our menu from that magical afternoon in the forest. This picnic travels beautifully and offers enough complex flavors to please adults—and enough sweetness to delight the kids. These recipes are easy to modify, are incredibly versatile, and come together quickly; I come back to them again and again for our quick spontaneous day trips.

STRAWBERRY SALAD WITH MINT + CINNAMON

We serve this as a sweet side salad, but it makes a rather delicious topping as well. Try it over biscuits or waffles in the morning or ice cream in the evening.

SERVES 8

2 tablespoons sugar
1 teaspoon cinnamon
3 sprigs of fresh mint, minced
2 pints strawberries, hulled and halved

1. Sift the sugar and cinnamon together until thoroughly combined. Add the sugar mixture and half of the mint to the strawberries and toss to coat. Cover and refrigerate for at least 30 minutes. Garnish with the remaining mint just before serving.

COCONUT CURRY CHICKEN SANDWICHES

We've been pretty adventurous with introducing our kids to a variety of flavors and cuisines. If your tastes run more traditional, simply omit the raisins, spices, and coconut butter from this recipe.

SERVES 8

½ cup raisins
1 cup boiling water
Organic rotisserie chicken,
    deboned and shredded

2 tablespoons fresh mint, minced
8 potato buns, for serving
Field greens, for serving

FOR THE DRESSING

½ cup full-fat Greek yogurt

2 tablespoons mayonnaise

1 tablespoon Dijon mustard

2 teaspoons fresh minced garlic

¼ cup melted coconut butter

½ teaspoon lemon juice

1 teaspoon coriander

⅛ teaspoon cumin

⅛ teaspoon cloves

¼ teaspoon chili powder

1. Add the raisins to the cup of boiling water and let stand for 10 minutes. Drain and set aside.

2. Make the dressing: whisk together the yogurt, mayonnaise, mustard, garlic, coconut butter, lemon juice, coriander, cumin, cloves, and chili powder.

3. Add the chicken to the dressing and toss until thoroughly coated. Mix in the raisins and mint. Fill eight potato buns with the chicken salad and top with the greens.

GARAM MASALA + PEANUT BUTTER COOKIES WITH CHOCOLATE CHUNKS

I've been making my grandmother Helen's peanut butter and chocolate chip cookies since I was ten years old. But when my friends Mark and Jenna of Whimsy and Spice allowed me to taste test their new Massaman Peanut Butter Sandwich Cookie several years ago, I knew what Gram's cookies needed next time I baked a few dozen.

1 cup butter, at room temperature

1¼ cup peanut butter, preferably creamy Jif

1 cup sugar

½ cup honey

2 organic eggs

½ teaspoon vanilla

2½ cups flour

2 teaspoons garam masala

1 teaspoon baking soda

1 teaspoon baking powder

1 cup chocolate chips, coarsely chopped

1. Preheat the oven to 350°F. Beat the butter and peanut butter together with a hand mixer. Add the sugar and mix until well blended. Add honey and mix.

2. Whisk the eggs and vanilla together in a small bowl. Add the egg mixture to the butter mixture and incorporate well. In another bowl, whisk the flour, garam masala, baking soda, and baking powder together. Slowly stir the dry mixture into the wet mixture. Scrape the bottom of the bowl several times to ensure all of the dry is properly mixed into the wet. Stir in the chocolate chips.

3. Place the dough in the refrigerator for up to 30 minutes.

4. Prepare baking sheets with parchment paper. Using a small ice cream scoop or tablespoon, create equal-sized balls of dough. Place them on the baking sheet about 2 inches apart. Return the dough to the fridge between each sheeting. Do not flatten the dough with a fork or any other means. Bake for 13 minutes or until edges just begin to turn gold. Let the cookies stand for about 5 minutes before transferring to a cooling rack.

PART FOUR

HOME AGAIN

Coming home. It's likely the most bittersweet moment we experience when traveling. As the days of blissful road wandering wind down and you move across the landscape homeward bound, there's a part of you that can't wait for the embrace of your own soft bed, a home-cooked meal in your sun-drenched kitchen, and the comfort of daily routine. But that other part of your heart, the one whose voice may have a bit more power, is asking, "Do we really have to go back already?" Thankfully, though reluctantly, there is always the road home.

You are aware of how much travel changes you. You are inspired to recreate dishes you tasted and new adventures you've experienced. If you have a family, you've likely found that it also changes your children. It helps transform them into curious and enlightened little beings. They too carry home a world of inspiration and ideas from the road. In this section you will find ideas for projects that allow you to live with that vacation long after the car has rolled back into the driveway. Creating physical representations of those wonderful memories on the road will not only serve as a reminder of what a great time was had, but will also keep the desire to do it all over again very much alive.

13

PHOTO ORGANIZATION

THE MOST TREASURED OF TRAVEL mementos are likely the photographs you took on your journey. While it can be overwhelming to think about going through those hundreds of files, let alone turning them into a keepsake, you can take a few steps to make the whole process incredibly rewarding.

Digital cameras have changed everything. From the way we photograph to the way we process and print our photographs, they've made taking pictures on vacation a much easier endeavor. However, as simple as it is to shoot, it's just as easy to forget what you've photographed. As a professional photographer, I created a rule for myself to sit down and pull everything I plan to edit into its own desktop folder the day I shot it. When you're on the road, however, this is a far from feasible plan of action. Even if you're traveling with your laptop and camera card reader, you will certainly lack the time (and possibly desire) to sift through all of those files.

Set aside some time once you've settled in again at home—after the laundry is caught up, after you feel at home again—to make yourself some coffee or tea and plug in that camera card. It's easy to think that you should save every photograph from your time on the road, but be mindful as you start sorting through the images. Some shots will obviously be problematic: they are blown out or overexposed, way too dark, too blurry, maybe a truly unflattering expression was captured; delete these. There is no reason to keep a photograph you don't love and feel connected to. Once you've deleted unwanted photos, I recommend organizing the remaining images in a way that feels easy to you, such as by location or by date. Whatever you find that works, create your folders and save your files appropriately.

⊙ PRINTING PHOTOS

While the most popular and expeditious way to share your vacation photos with friends and family is by posting online, do not forgot to print them. This used to be something we never had to consider, of course there were prints when we dropped off our film at the lab. Now, more photographs live online than on the mantelpiece at home. Remember, they are physical keepsakes.

Once the files are ready, you can print on demand.

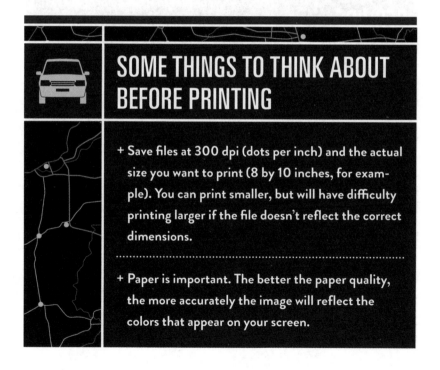

SOME THINGS TO THINK ABOUT BEFORE PRINTING

+ Save files at 300 dpi (dots per inch) and the actual size you want to print (8 by 10 inches, for example). You can print smaller, but will have difficulty printing larger if the file doesn't reflect the correct dimensions.

+ Paper is important. The better the paper quality, the more accurately the image will reflect the colors that appear on your screen.

IF USING A PROFESSIONAL PRINTING SERVICE, *ALSO* NOTE THE FOLLOWING

+ Most printers will ask for .jpg files. These files tend to be smaller than .tif or .psd files. However, for the longevity and health of your image files, save edited images as a .tif or .psd as well because they retain more image and color information than a .jpg.

+ Save your files in RGB color space, as that is what most printers require for correct color calibration.

+ Some printers may ask you to calibrate your monitor to ensure the colors are correct. You can find instructions online to walk you through this easy process for your specific computer.

+ Be sure not to select the option to have your files color-corrected. This often results in strange and unexpected color shifts.

 **PHOTO BOOKS**

Photo books, once simple scrapbooks, are now full-fledged self-published beauties. You don't need to worry about the archival quality of the glue or the page dividers—just how you want to lay out that one-of-a-kind family publication and how many copies to have printed. You'll find later that paging through at leisure is always an acute reminder of how wonderful that journey truly was—and it will likely inspire you to get back on the road sooner rather than later.

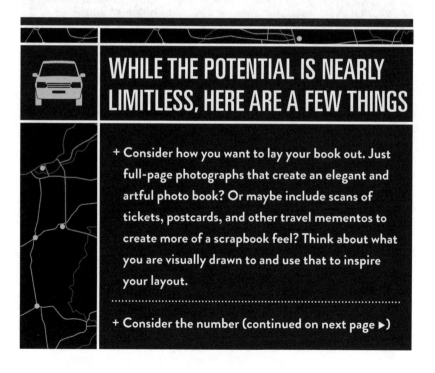

WHILE THE POTENTIAL IS NEARLY LIMITLESS, HERE ARE A FEW THINGS

+ Consider how you want to lay your book out. Just full-page photographs that create an elegant and artful photo book? Or maybe include scans of tickets, postcards, and other travel mementos to create more of a scrapbook feel? Think about what you are visually drawn to and use that to inspire your layout.

+ Consider the number (continued on next page ▶)

of books you want to create. A small book for each road trip, maybe? Or save your photos and create a tome of all your travels at the end of each year.

+ The resources section lists some of the companies that can print your photo books. Most have easy-to-use software that you download to your computer. You then select a template of your book design, upload your images, and place your order. In about one to two weeks, your book will arrive. It's really that easy. If you are Photoshop-savvy, you can layer text and those aforementioned tickets over some of your images.

◉ DISPLAY IDEAS

Books are wonderful mementos to recall your time on the road, but here are a few more ideas on what to do with your printed photographs:

+ My absolute favorite way to remember a road trip is by tucking photographs in unexpected places all over our home—especially in the corners of artwork and mirrors.

....

+ Create small collages using three to five images throughout your home with washi tape on a previously blank patch of wall space.

....

+ An 8-by-10-inch or 11-by-14-inch print is perfectly respectable. But don't be afraid to go big. Remember when we talked about editing and saving your files for printing? Just ensure that the image you've chosen is saved large enough to print that size. I have a 40-by-60-inch photograph in our home that I shot on a trip to Paris—it makes a real statement and I smile every single time I see it. (continued on next page ▶)

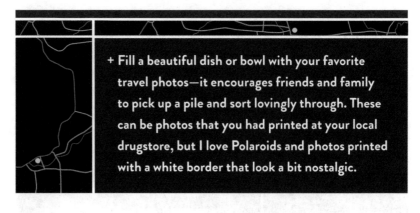

+ Fill a beautiful dish or bowl with your favorite travel photos—it encourages friends and family to pick up a pile and sort lovingly through. These can be photos that you had printed at your local drugstore, but I love Polaroids and photos printed with a white border that look a bit nostalgic.

⊙ DISPLAY IDEAS FOR KIDS

Creating travel displays for children helps kids remember and cherish your time together on the road. It often surprises me how much my girls remember of some of our first travels together when they were little. It surprises me even more when they recall seemingly long-forgotten memories with visual prompts. Photographs, drawings, even saved menus and brochures can conjure all sorts of tales from your little ones, and it's always fascinating to hear how their perspective of their experience changes over the years.

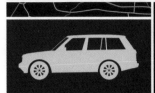

A FEW ACTIVITIES YOU CAN DO TOGETHER THAT WILL HELP KEEP THOSE MEMORIES ALIVE

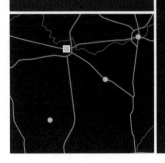

+ Purchase a large frame (30 by 40 inches, for example) and arrange smaller images in a grid fashion that tell a chronological tale of your trip. Children will love being able to physically touch these memories and help you arrange them on the paper. Ask them to help you remember what came first, second, and so on.

+ Print photos on copy paper at home and sit your child down with a stack of them and scissors—work on a fun travel collage together. Allow them to draw all over it and add details, you might be truly surprised by what you end up with.

+ Make a collage of photos on a blank wall. Allowing your child to help arrange them will make it feel incredibly special, as if they are creating a piece of installation art for their home.

Take the time sooner rather than later to organize your photos. You want your recollections to be fresh and accurate when sifting through and organizing all of your files. We often feel as if we need a vacation from our vacation when we return home. But by finding a quiet moment and a little time to reflect on the collected moments from your travels, you will relive that feeling of freedom, abandon, and escape, and remember how important it is to always seek out adventure.

14

—

COLLECTIONS AND KEEPSAKES

ONE OF MY FIRST ROAD TRIPS across the United States was from Nebraska to California. I have since retraced that road many times, but I will never forget my first experience watching the Plains rise up into the Rockies then slumber once again to create the quiet desert. I was six years old, and at every pit stop, I collected a rock. Some of those rocks very well may have been pieces of asphalt, but I didn't care. I was collecting something that represented my voyage across America. Collections can be as inexpensive and simple as my roadside rocks to seeking out a handmade bowl at an antique store in each city or state of your journey. Let your passions guide you here. This is something you want to display in your home, so collect things that resonate with your soul and speak to who you are. Here are a few ideas to get you started.

ANTIQUES AND HANDMADE GOODS

Do you always find yourself drawn to ceramic pitchers hand-crafted by local artisans? Or maybe you're having a passionate love affair with vintage barware. Seek out those items every time you are on the road. Every piece will hold a story about your travels that you will remember forever. Grouping collections together on a shelf in your home is an especially powerful display method—and always seems to invite conversation.

JEWELRY

I've collected jewelry when traveling since my early twenties when I was living and working in Europe. I can look into my jewelry box and tell you not only where I purchased every piece, but give that bauble a sense of atmosphere and higher purpose. Maybe bracelets are your favorite piece to wear or earrings—focus on what you love. When my daughters were born, I started buying small silver cuffs or silver charms to gift them one day when they are older. I hope they find that those mementos recall the wonderful times we've shared on the road.

SOUVENIRS

There are some quintessential travel souvenirs that you can find at nearly every pit stop you make. Spoons, magnets, ball caps. These are fun and pretty easy items to seek out and collect. But if you want a real challenge and to add a little bit more meaning to the process, take it a step further. Instead of the mass-produced state spoons, seek out a beautiful vintage silver-plated spoon in antique stores from every state or city; you're sure to find unique handmade magnets at artisan markets and maybe limit yourself to ball caps only from microbreweries. Remember, follow your passion.

⦿ PAPER

Tickets, boarding passes, subway maps—all sorts of paper will make a fantastic travel collage. And as discussed in part 2, paper ephemera is a fantastic way to add another layer of depth and interest to your travel journaling process. Posters are another favorite; we try to purchase one at every museum we come across. One of the easiest and least expensive souvenirs to collect is a postcard. Purchase one that you love at every stop—maybe sticking to a theme such as a vintage aesthetic or a predominately blue foreground—and create a collage of them at home.

⦿ THE OLD STANDBYS

We often find charm in nostalgia. Mugs, key chains, shot glasses, magnets, snow globes, seashells, charms, and matchbooks. There's a reason every tourist shop is jam packed with these kinds of trinkets: people buy them. If that's what you love, go for it!

A FEW MORE IDEAS TO GET YOUR COLLECTION STARTED

+ Ceramic mugs or bowls

+ Wooden spoons

+ Pens or pencils from memorable hotels

+ Large crystal specimens from rock shops

+ T-shirts that showcase local teams or businesses

+ Holiday ornaments (they don't have to be traditional ornaments, just something you could hang
on your tree)

+ Local cookbooks

+ Menus or coasters from your favorite dining experiences

(continued on next page▶)

+ Textiles (blankets, table linens, or wraps)

+ Vintage decorative plates

+ Prints by local artists

+ Books by local authors

⦿ COLLECTIONS FOR KIDS

Collections can foster pride and devotion in children. It helps give them a sense of purpose on the road. And because they realize pieces of their collections are not easily found every day, they learn to take care of something that they've had a direct hand in building. When deciding what to collect, let your children choose. If it is something that will be difficult to locate, talk to them and set realistic expectations about what you'll find together. If it's something a bit less challenging, like collecting seashells, have a conversation about the importance of not hoarding every shell their toes find in the surf, but collecting beautiful specimens with intention. Finally, creating collections can be the ideal sneaky learning tool. Not sure what kind of seashell that is? Check out a book from the library and learn about the different species. Make a wish list of the type of shells you'd like to seek out on this trip. Certain types of shells are more abundant on particular coasts, so not only is your child learning to create a special collection of their own, but a touch of marine biology and geology to boot.

What to collect is a limitless conversation. Just remember to look to your children for guidance when creating and displaying their collections. If they have specific passions, be sure to look at ways that you can somehow create a collection out of those interests. If the collection is more for mama or papa than child, they will lose interest rather quickly and never really invest in the process. Remember that you can always start your own collection as well. Here are some ideas to get you started.

 POSTCARDS

These will make a fantastic wall collage or flip book. You can have your children collect postcards at every stop or hone in on a specific idea, like only at state parks. The collection can be visually cohesive by collecting vintage-looking postcards or just let them choose whatever they think is the most colorful and appealing to their eye. Display postcards on a wall in their room; make it extra special by arranging them in a shape (like a heart or arrow). They can also be placed in small frames and hung together, glued or taped into a journal with notes about each stop, or made into a flip book by punching holes in each card and securing them together with metal rings—they can add notes to the back of each card.

⊙ ROCKS

Collecting rocks was always my favorite. This allows for another wonderful learning opportunity for your children as well. Rocks and minerals can be lined for display on an open shelf or placed in glass jars. If they are more prone to picking up smooth pebbles, paint them in fun colors and patterns and mark each on the bottom with a Sharpie pen noting where they were located.

⊙ SEASHELLS

Shells can be displayed much like rocks and minerals. When adding them to glass containers or jars, I love the idea of including a bit of sand from the beach where the shells were found as well and marking each jar by the name of the beach. For both shell and rock collecting, it's great to travel with a Sharpie and box of Ziplocs, allowing for easy classification reminders when home.

⊙ PENCILS/PENS

This is a great idea for kids who love to draw and write. Most state parks, roadside attractions, hotels, and the like will have pencils and/or pens with their names marked onto the side. This can be a fun and rather useful item to collect. If you'd rather not use them, display them in pencil cups made of maps (simply a recycled tin can with a cut map glued on as a label). Or glue pencils to a piece of reclaimed wood to create a lasting keepsake for the wall—just be sure to leave room so the collection can grow.

 FLOWERS/PLANTS

It may be difficult to fathom how you can collect live plants while traveling, but with a little prep work, it's easy. While travel-friendly and inexpensive pressing kits are available (see the resources), you can also improvise by putting any large heavy book in your trunk along with enough pieces of wax paper to place under and on top of your finds so they won't stick to the pages of your book. Depending on the type and size of flora you are pressing, it may take between a few days and a few weeks to completely flatten and dry. Once flowers are pressed and dry, you can frame them with small, artful tags noting the species and location found, or crush the petals to make a filling for a very special little sleepy time pillow. This project will likely need parental guidance, as pressed flowers are very fragile.

BOOKS

Regional books, especially children's books, make a lasting collection of keepsakes that you can pass down through generations. Gift shops at state parks and local attractions (like a zoo or historic home) often have collections of books for both adults and children written about the area.

A word of warning for adults and children alike: Collections can quickly grow out of control. It's important to be thoughtful in selecting both what you wish to collect, and building the collection itself. Over the years I have become more aligned with a minimalistic approach in most aspects of my life, from the toys and kitchen tools in our home to my wardrobe. It took me many years to get to this place—it's a constant work in progress—and it has brought me such peace. But I realize we do not all desire a similar lifestyle. When considering collections, be honest with yourself: Will you take the time to care for and display your collection with the intention of passing it down through your family? Or will it likely end up in a donation box in a few years—or worse, a landfill? Be mindful of not only your desires but the world around you as well. Lastly, think about what you are comfortable spending on your collection; the idea is to collect with intention and purpose, not to dip deeply into your travel budget.

MAPS

Is any other visual more strongly associated with travel than a map? In many ways, traditional paper maps have taken an artful backseat to all of our electrical accouterments that tell us in a soothing voice how many feet until the next turn. But we always have a paper map or atlas on hand; it soothes my paranoid what-if-we-lose-signal soul. Maps can be rather straightforward in terms of design or incredibly artful. Either way, they are perfect keepsakes to remember your recent road trip. Most service stations and bookstores carry maps, but local artisan shops often have creative ways to execute this same concept. Decide if you are collecting for practicality or display purposes.

The most essential "thing" you bring home from any trip is, of course, your memories and new experiences. Anita Desai, an Indian novelist and professor at Massachusetts Institute of Technology, proclaimed, "Wherever you go becomes a part of you somehow." It alters the way you see yourself, the way you see the world. The gift of travel bestows upon you the ability to see your home and the people in your life in an entirely new way. Do not discount this great keepsake of your journey. Talk about your memories with those you shared them, and keep the flame

SOME IDEAS ON HOW TO DISPLAY YOUR MAPS

+ Purchase a large wall map of the United States and use pushpins of one color to show the places you've visited, and others colors to note the places you'd love to go next (you could even color-code those desires by family member).

....

+ Don't limit yourself to pins: add small printed photos from your travels or postcards to note places on your wall maps as well.

....

+ Create a wall of framed maps—varying sizes, vintages, and locations—to represent your favorite family road trips. Or cover an interior wall with maps creating a custom travel wallpaper.

....

+ Use a map as the mat frame for a photograph taken in that location.

....

+ Get your scissors out! Cut out shapes (continued on next page ▶)

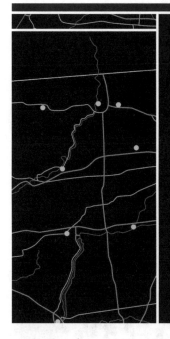

from a city or subway map that you recently used on a trip, and fold into paper airplanes or butterflies to hang all over the ceiling of your child's room. With a bit of string or glue, you can also create a map mobile.

....

+ Think of maps as you would any ephemera: use them to decoupage a pencil canister, make them part of a 2-D or 3-D collage, or write or draw about your travels directly on the map to create a one-of-a-kind piece of art.

of desire to do more, see more, and be more alive. When I took my oldest daughter to Greece when she was eleven, our relationship was being tested in ways that are a normal trajectory for the ache of adolescence. But we talked then about how we would remember that trip—how when we were angry or frustrated with each other, we would take a deep breath, hold each other, and talk about Greece. Memories are the greatest of souvenirs, and truly, the only thing you need to bring home.

RESOURCES

 **GET INSPIRED**

These books will inspire you to see the world—or maybe just a familiar stretch of highway—in a new way.

1,000 Place to See Before You Die by Patricia Schultz

The Alchemist by Paulo Coelho

The Art of Travel by Alain de Botton

Atlas Obscura: An Explorer's Guide to the World's Hidden Wonders by Joshua Foer and Dylan Thuras

Blue Highways by William Least Heat-Moon

Canyon Solitude: A Woman's Solo River Journey through the Grand Canyon by Patricia McCairen

Cross Country: Fifteen Years and 90,000 Miles on the Roads with Interstates of America and Lewis and Clark by Robert Sullivan

Eat, Pray, Love by Elizabeth Gilbert

A Field Guide to Getting Lost by Rebecca Solnit

How to Be an Explorer of the World: Portable Life Museum by Keri Smith

Life is a Trip: The Transformative Magic of Travel by Judith Fein

The Lonely Planet Anthology: True Stories from the World's Best Writers by Lonely Planet

The Lost Continent: Travels in Small-Town America by Bill Bryson

On the Road by Jack Kerouac

Road Trip USA: Cross-Country Adventures on America's Two-Lane Highways by Jamie Jensen

The Travels of Marco Polo by Marco Polo

Travels with Charley in Search of America by John Steinbeck

A Walk in the Woods: Rediscovering America on the Appalachian Trail by Bill Bryson

The Wander Society by Keri Smith

The Weetzie Bat Books by Francesca Lia Block

Wild: From Lost to Found on the Pacific Crest Trail by Cheryl Strayed

Wreck This Journal by Keri Smith

 TO HELP YOU ON YOUR WAY

This list of websites will help you do everything from daydream and pack for your road trip to find the best places to eat, shop, and sleep.

Airbnb has redefined the way we travel. Hotels, campsites, and friends' couches start looking a little ho-hum next to the options available on this wildly popular site. With over 1.5 million listings in more than 34,000 cities, there is an apartment, home, or even a tree house with your name on it somewhere in this world: www.airbnb.com.

Artifact Uprising is my absolute favorite printing service. What began as a seamless service to upload your Instagram photos directly from your phone for printing has evolved into a full-service artisan printing business. Large format prints and calendars are some of their latest offerings, but I still love their printed books—an easy and truly elegant way to keep your travel memories always within reach: www.artifactuprising.com.

Blurb is another favorite book printer and what I used to self-publish my books in my early days as an author. It's incredibly user friendly and now offers a variety of new formats including magazines and e-books: www.blurb.com.

Eat Your World currently offers dining suggestions for over 130 locations around the globe. It is user-sourced and growing in content every day. A wonderful resource for finding memorable meals, creative cocktails, and microbrews when traveling abroad: www.eatyourworld.com.

Foursquare is an app designed to make you feel like a local . . . even when you're miles from home. With over 75 million tips from travelers and locals alike, the app helps you locate the best restaurants, shopping, and nightlife of any given location. Its rise in popularity has given way to Foursquare Swarm, a game to connect with those aforementioned locals. Search or download at: www.foursquare.com.

Her Packing List is a pretty thorough resource for packing absolutely anything and going anywhere. Weekend at your in-laws? Covered. Twelve-day hike across Bhutan? Pretty sure that's covered as well. Provides wonderful insight into how to pack, luggage and bag reviews, packing lists, and tips for packing less and enjoying more: www.herpackinglist.com. (A great packing app can be found at www.packpnt.com.)

Hipcamp wants you to get outdoors . . . and sleep there. Featuring over 280,000 campsites across the United States, the site has become a go-to guide for campers. Hipcamp showcases camping locations in public/national parks and grounds and also offers a comprehensive guide to private land camping opportunities as well: www.hipcamp.com.

Home Science Tools offers a variety of road-friendly kits for children to explore the world around them while traveling. The Plant Press Kit and the Young Naturalist's Backpack Kit are my favorites: www.homesciencetools.com.

Hotel Tonight can be a lifesaver. You can plan every moment of your trip and still experience unexpected hiccups. If you find yourself in need of a hotel immediately, this app specifically targets properties in your current location with availability. Download the app at: www.hoteltonight.com.

iExit is an app designed especially for American road trips. Gas stations, restaurants, and cafés must pay a fee to be featured on interstate road signs, as such, they do not give you a clear picture of what's ahead. When used while driving U.S. interstates, the app automatically reads your location and gives you updates about where to pit stop at the upcoming exits: www. iexitapp.com.

Open Bay is an app that allows you to diagnose car problems and locates nearby mechanics based on your location. I recommend always traveling with roadside assistance, but this is a great tool to have in case of an emergency: www.openbay.com.

Photobooth.net promises to be "the most comprehensive photo booth resource on the internet." I love their "Locator" feature— type in a city name and it will generate a list of known photo booth locations. Best souvenir ever: www.photobooth.net.

Pinterest is sort of the holy grail of visual inspiration online these days. Use it as a planning resource to find packable food ideas, journaling tips, and games and activities to keep the little ones busy in the back seat. Just type your wish into the Pinterest search bar and await a plethora of inspiration: www.pinterest.com.

Roadfood is a comprehensive guide to local dining while traveling across America. Forget fast food and chain restaurants, the best way to discover the authenticity of a town or city is in their local dining establishments. This website allows you to search by location or food type and even features city food tours—hand-picked hot spots that can't be missed. You'll likely not come across a "fine-dining" experience when using this tool, but I can promise you tasting adventures await: www.roadfood.com.

Roadside America is both a website and mobile app helping you discover the most obscure and unique places on the highway. From the Cadillac Ranch in Amarillo, Texas, featuring a sculpture garden of graffiti-clad and upended Caddys, to a museum dedicated to the ambush of infamous outlaws Bonnie and Clyde in Gibsland, Louisiana, the site offers detailed descriptions of each attraction, hours, associated costs, and directions: www.roadsideamerica.com.

Roadtrippers is a fantastic resource (and app) for planning a trip across America—particularly off the beaten path. The site's predesigned road guides (such as Boston to Miami: Road Trip Down the Atlantic Coast) suggests number of days on the road, what to see, where to eat and stay, and recommendations about the best time of year to travel that given route. The site also allows you to design your own trip for a total streamlined process: www.roadtrippers.com.

Travel Diaries allows you to journal digitally and share your adventure with the world. With an online platform that looks like a real open book on a table, you can add text, photos, and maps to your diary on the go; then share the stories via links. It allows you to play with layout, style, and text, and—coolest of all—the company will print your diary upon completion: www.traveldiariesapp.com.

Travel Mamas is a website offering a plethora of advice on traveling with children. Featuring inspiring family travel stories from all around the United States and the world over, the site also serves as a fantastic reference for the ins and outs of being on the road with the kids. The packing lists on this site are especially well thought out: www.travelmamas.com.

TV Food Maps is another road food web source, but the site only features dining spots that have been featured on . . . you guessed it, television. Featuring restaurants from nearly fifty shows such as *Bizarre Eats* and Anthony Bourdain's *The Layover*, you can search by show or location. The site has exploded in popularity and now offers a user-friendly mobile app—perfect for your road warrior days: www.tvfoodmaps.com.

Woo Junior was designed to provide hours of entertainment for kids. Since Internet connections are often difficult to come by while on the road, check out the "Printables" section. Print travel games, Mad Libs, and coloring sheets before you hit the road. I always pack the kids a clipboard for such activities: www.woojr.com.

ABOUT THE AUTHOR

HAVING STUDIED INTERIOR DESIGN AT the Art Institute of Pittsburgh and art history at Arizona State University, Jen CK Jacobs worked for nearly ten years as an editorial photographer. Her photography and styling work has been exhibited throughout North America and is held in private collections across the globe; her clients include Chronicle Books, Roost Books, *Martha Stewart Living*, Delta Airlines, *Food & Wine*, Food Network, and *Kinfolk* magazine among others. Her work has been featured in countless publications including *TIME, Lucky, Redbook, Marie Claire, O, The Oprah Magazine, Refinery29, Daily Candy, VOGUE* online, and *Bon Appétit* online. She has authored several books including *Instant Love: How to Make Magic and Memories with Polaroids, Photographing Your Children: A Handbook of Style and Instruction, Gem and Stone: Jewels of Earth, Sea, and Sky,* and *The Circadian Tarot: A Daily Companion for Divination and Illumination* (all under the name Jen Altman).

Jen lives just outside of Asheville, North Carolina, with her husband and six children.